Every Life Has A Story And This Is Mine

Jack A. Pritchard, M.D.

Chairman of Obstetrics and Gynecology
University of Texas Southwestern Medical School
1955 – 1970

Foreword, Epilogue, and footnotes by
Judy A. Wagers, Editor

Private printing: November 2013
First printing: January 2014

Publisher:
CreateSpace Independent Publishing Platform*
Charleston, SC

Cover Photographs

FRONT: *Jack A. Pritchard, M.D.,* 1988 from Dallas Medical Images, News and Publications Collection (nap_00070) and the OB/Gyn Archives

BACK: *Jack A. Pritchard, M.D., camping in Arizona mountains* circa 1990. Pritchard Family Photo courtesy of Signe Allen Pritchard

Pritchard, Jack Arthur, 1921—2003 [author]
    Every Life Has a Story And This Is Mine — 2nd edition
    1. Biography and Autobiography—Personal Memoirs

Wagers, Judy Anne, 1943— [editor]

ISBN: 1495264246
ISBN–13: 978-1495264245

For
Signe Allen Pritchard
whose love and encouragement brought us this
story[§]

OB/GYN Archives – David Gresham
Photographer

Signe Allen Pritchard
November 28, 2001

[§] The first printing of *Every Life Has A Story And This Is Mine* in November 2013 was a surprise for Signe Allen Pritchard's 90th birthday. Without Signe, this manuscript might never have been written. And once written, might never have been published. Happy Birthday and thanks, Signe!

Contents

Foreword

During 2001, Jack Pritchard wrote *Every Life Has A Story And This Is Mine*. The manuscript, typed by Lynne McDonnell, was 30 single-spaced pages in length and had a picture of Dr. Pritchard below the title on the first page.

Dr. Pritchard's original, unedited manuscript is reproduced in this book along with the original photo of Dr. Pritchard. Additional pictures have been inserted from family and departmental archives; from the UT Southwestern Medical Center Library Digital Repository's Dallas Medical Images; and from the Royal College of Obstetricians and Gynaecologists. Permission to use the photographs is gratefully acknowledged, and sources are credited in the captions.

To preserve the integrity of the original manuscript, all editorial additions are confined to the Foreword, Editor's Addendum, Epilogue, and footnotes. Footnotes are used to define medical terms for the lay reader, to provide references to publications mentioned in the text, and to add contextual commentary.[§]

This edition is dedicated to the memory of Jack Arthur Pritchard, M.D., who brought science to obstetrics and gynecology. His contributions forever changed how women's health care is practiced and affected the lives of women everywhere. Yet, he never forgot that his patients were women with names and stories of their own to tell.

Judy A. Wagers, Editor
Dallas, Texas
September 1, 2012

www.utsouthwestern.edu/obgyn-academics
www.utsouthwestern.org/obgyn

[§] After receiving a copy of the book as a surprise for her 90th birthday, Signe Pritchard enthusiastically decided to publish it. Prior to the book's release to the public in January 2014, the editorial additions were updated through 2013. – Editor

EVERY LIFE HAS A STORY
AND THIS IS MINE

Jack A. Pritchard, M.D.

OB/GYN Archives – 1988

A currently popular television program is so titled. I have watched several presentations and wondered if this might be true for my life. With the strong help of Signe, my wife of 57 years, I set out to review my life from conception in 1920 until fully retired from the University of Texas Southwestern Medical Center at Dallas in 1990.

From 1955 until 1970 I was Chairman of the Department of Obstetrics and Gynecology (Ob/Gyn) at the University of Texas Southwestern Medical Center and Chief of OB/Gyn at Parkland Memorial Hospital. In 1970, I relinquished the dual appointment and then functioned primarily as Chief of Obstetrics at Parkland Hospital. In addition from 1969-1973, I established and served as the Director of the Greater Dallas Maternal Health and Family Planning Program.

My conclusion after compiling this review is, "Yes, there is an interesting – even informative story – and it might be of value to some other individuals." Remember, you can learn from the mistakes of others!

THE EVOLUTION OF AN ACADEMIC OBSTETRICIAN
(Compiled at the insistence of my wife of 57 years)

Where to start? Why not begin with my mother's[1] first pregnancy in which I was the intrauterine occupant. Did it have any influence on my career in obstetrics? From my father's[2] description of events that occurred, my mother developed generalized swelling, then lost consciousness, and finally suffered generalized shaking. He related these events to me long after my birth. In the way of "treatment", he said the doctor urged that she not eat any pork and limit water intake even though she complained of thirst. She survived and obviously so did I.[3] Did these developments typical of eclampsia[4] play

---

[1] His mother, Marguerite McKee, was born about 1902 in Hinckley, Ohio.

[2] His father, George Frederick Pritchard, was born about 1900 in Grand River, Ohio.

[3] Jack Arthur Pritchard was born July 25, 1921 in Painesville, Ohio.
Named after General Edward Paine, Painesville had a population of 7,272 in 1920. By the 1930 census, the town had grown to 10,944. The area was settled in the early 1800s and was part of the Connecticut Land Company's Western Reserve land holdings.
http://www.findagrave.com/cgi-bin/fg.cgi?page=gr&GRid=14189339

[4] Eclampsia – the final and most severe stage of a prenatal complication frequently referred to as *toxemia of pregnancy*. Preeclampsia-eclampsia is characterized by high blood pressure and a high level of protein in the urine. If left untreated, seizures, coma, and death can occur in the final *eclamptic* stage.

any role in my ultimate career as an academic obstetrician? Probably not, but let's look.

From birth until 6 years of age, I was exposed to some serious medical complications. My younger brother died from a "telescoped bowel," now called "intussusception."[5] A surgeon from Cleveland 30 miles away came to Painesville, Ohio and operated unsuccessfully. Soon thereafter I developed very similar symptomatology and physical findings. Again from Cleveland came the surgeon who promptly operated and told my father my belly was filled with pus that had to be drained. For what seemed to be an eternity the drains were left in. I had a special night nurse whose only job from my standpoint was to squeeze my belly from side to side to expel pus. She was actually a nice person most of the time who stayed beyond her 12-hour night shift to try to get me well. Red Grange was then a famous football player, and she would read to me about him and help me cut out pictures of Red galloping down the field.

Finally, they removed the drains but only after warning my folks, and especially me, that if I were to exercise the incision just might open up and they described the dire consequences. My young surgeon, I learned much later, was specializing in orthopedic surgery. I guess that gave him the right to be vigorous with my treatment. The abdominal scar and the healed drain sites remain quite prominent 75 years later and always incite comments whenever a physical examination is performed, and, no incisional hernia developed! Apparently, these events played no discernible role in my evolution as an obstetrician nor did the birth of my sister, who is 7 years younger than I.[6]

The death of my brother, referred to above, and my mother's emergency surgery for what was most likely an ectopic pregnancy,[7] was almost more than my parents could cope with. It seemed as if a

---

[5] In this medical condition, one part of the intestine collapses into another much as the pieces of a telescope slide into one another.

[6] Shirley A. Pritchard was two at the time of the 1930 census.

[7] Ectopic pregnancy – abnormal pregnancy where the fertilized egg attaches outside the uterus, frequently in the fallopian tube; sometimes called a *tubal pregnancy*.

cloud of doom hovered over our house! Actually it was over more than one house as we moved to try to downscale expenses.

Somehow, I again became the target of more surgery of "minor" nature: a tonsillectomy and a circumcision. I clearly remember the painful first few postoperative days and even years later still appreciated the discomfort that the newborns I was circumcising were certainly suffering. (Later on I attempted to substitute a simple small vertical slit in the foreskin that provided for easy retraction.)

So far my medical experiences summarized above provided no stimulus to my wanting to become a physician. Maybe in my dreams another Red Grange or Charles Lindbergh who had flown alone across the Atlantic, but not a doctor. It should be pointed out, however, that the Great Depression was widespread and most of the country's families were engaged in Herculean efforts to provide food, clothing, and shelter, not advanced education. My father was a part-time brakeman and part-time yardmaster on a branch line of the B&O Railroad. It was almost totally a freight line that hauled coal from mines in West Virginia to the small Lake Erie docks at Fairport Harbor, Ohio, where it was then transported up the Great Lakes by steamboat. The same or similar steamboats would then bring iron ore from the upper Great Lakes to docks on the lower Great Lakes where blast furnaces converted it into steel. Whenever the market for steel dropped, the small ports and their ships and rail lines were the first to be shut down. Unfortunately, my father's work and, in turn, income depended on one of these small coal-iron ore operations. At times other jobs would appear but would not be available to men. Two spring "vacations" I worked planting rosebush cuttings at a local nursery for 90 cents a day (10 cents an hour, 9 hours a day). I was hired while men like my father who sought work were turned down by the owner who said it was embarrassing to hire grown men for 10 cents an hour. At lunch break, we would compare sandwiches to see how many had U.S. Government distributed cheese. The majority usually did.

A paper route became available and it was offered to me. I gladly accepted even though it increased the walk to school and home to 4 plus miles. This lasted until the owner of the gas station where I picked up the papers demanded a lion's share of my skimpy profits. My route manager and the gas station owner engaged in verbal fisticuffs, and the result was my quitting.

I looked for another source of income and found it on Main Street in downtown Painesville, population 10,000. I worked one day a week – Saturday from 8:00 a.m. to 10:00 p.m. – in a low-price shoe store. I cleaned the store before opening and after closing. The shoe store was immediately adjacent to a one-man pharmacy. In those days, a pharmacist's only required training was by apprenticeship. On occasion, I would wash the drug store windows along with the shoe store's. This impressed the pharmacist. One day he asked me how much I made which was 25 cents an hour. He could not pay me more but he emphasized that I could "learn" from him and maybe one day become a pharmacist myself. I was enjoying high school chemistry and was also intrigued by all the glass bottles in the drug store, so I changed jobs.

By now I had forgotten the painful experience of getting my middle finger crushed between a bicycle wheel and chain some years before and its "treatment" by another local pharmacist. This happened when I was about 6 years old. I was attracted to a group of teenage boys who had a two-wheeled bicycle upside down on the grass and were hand peddling it swiftly. Then one would press the coaster brake to slow the wheel down. One of them dared me to do it. I did, but put my hand into the chain and spokes very briefly but not briefly enough. The distal phalanx[8] of my third finger on my left hand, including the joint, got chewed appreciably. I went home, we got into our Model T Ford and drove into town for help. Where? We went to the drug store where a friend of my dad and the most popular of the four town pharmacists worked. (More about him later.) Somehow the injury served to numb the finger as he cut off skin, pulled out the fingernail, poured on various liquids and compressed the phalanx back towards the normal, and put a big bandage over it. I think I was rewarded with an ice cream cone. Since the bandage stayed on for a long time and I needed to write in school, I was forced to learn to use

---

[8] Distal phalanx – the tip of the finger below the last joint.

my right hand though I had been totally left-handed up until then. As a result, I write with the right hand and can do surgery and sports as well as eat with either hand.

WHY PHARMACY?

As I progressed through high school[9] some thoughts as to college were occasionally mentioned at home. My father insisted that I try to go. "Somehow the family will find a way. We always have in the past!" He emphasized that whatever I did it should train me to fill one of the few vacant jobs available. He immediately extolled the virtues of pharmacy. The ready availability of a job appealed to me as well. Before I knew it, it was 1938, and I was enrolled at Ohio Northern University (ONU).[10] I had been a good to superior student in high school, and the alumnus who recruited me was a high school teacher of mine. She said there were a few scholarships available, and I would most likely qualify for one. Unfortunately, I did not. The administration did not provide any help financially. I was financially vulnerable but decided to at least start school. Things were cheap and I was determined. Also, I felt compelled to demonstrate to the administration that I had real potential, which I thought I did. I made straight A's from day one to the final quarter, after Pearl Harbor when I relaxed a bit.

As time went on I became more disenchanted with pharmacy. It was relatively easy to get a pharmacy job because few people were entering the specialty and more were dropping out. Though I was not overwhelmed by the intellectual capacity demonstrated by small-town doctors, by this time I recognized that medicine was a more challenging field. I began to analyze the possibility of going to medical school or at least graduate school and obtaining a Ph.D. in Pharmacology.

---

[9] Jack Pritchard attended Harvey High School in Painesville, Ohio, from 1934–1938, graduating in June.

[10] ONU—a private, coeducational university affiliated with the Methodist Church since 1899—was founded in 1871 by Henry Solomon Lehr. Located in Ada, Ohio, the university has five colleges—including a College of Pharmacy (established in 1885–1886).
http://www.onu.edu/about_onu/a_brief_history_of_onu

The pharmacy curriculum was not terribly hard, just rigid. Even so, I was allowed to either trade or to add on courses that hopefully would convince a medical school admissions committee or graduate school that I was sincere and that I was not an academic risk. By the beginning of my second year, I had established that I could master a tougher curriculum at the same time as that of pharmacy. For example, I took the hardest two courses for chemistry majors and made As in both. I also took physics, zoology, engineering calculus, and German. These courses at least would prepare me for graduate school.

MEDICAL COLLEGE APTITUDE TEST

My roommate spotted the announcement informing people that the Medical College Aptitude Test (MCAT) would be given shortly, and he thought I might be interested. I certainly was! He went with me to the office of the Head of the Biology Department who would be administering the test. The Biology Department Head laughed rather intensely when we told him we wanted to take the MCAT and implied that we would be doomed by poor performances. He had only one copy of the examination, but he finally said that if one of us wanted to take it, he could see no reason not to let us. My roommate and I flipped a coin. I won the toss! The Dean of the Biology Department continued to discourage my taking the test because of my lack of formal premedical preparation. Nonetheless I took the test.

In due time the Dean summoned me to his office to let me know that he had results of the MCAT. After a pause, he bluntly said, "Where do you want to go to medical school? You can get in most anywhere you apply." I did get in but it was not quite as easy as the Dean said.

The attack on Pearl Harbor brought major changes. Word was that the seniors at ONU, of which I was one, would be allowed to

Pritchard Family Photo

Jack A. Pritchard

Graduation Photo — 1942

Ohio Northern University

graduate a month early and then be immediately eligible for military duty.[11] Medical school was gone from my mind, as were the fellowships awarded me by the University of North Carolina and Purdue University Graduate Schools. I relaxed a bit academically, and my perfect grade point average of 3.0 dropped to 2.97.

The only questions seemed to be when and where I would go in the military. I talked to a naval recruiting officer who told me that I qualified for the rank of petty officer third class because of my degree in pharmacy. It turned out I did not qualify since I was not yet 21.

ACCEPTANCE TO MEDICAL SCHOOL – FINALLY

My mother encountered a friend of mine from my high school days, Russell Rizzo. During the course of the conversation, she learned he was in medical school at Case Western Reserve University.[12] She mentioned to him my desire to go to medical school. He

---

[11] Jack Pritchard attended Ohio Northern University from 1938–1942, graduating in May with a B.S. Degree in Pharmacy.

[12] When Dr. Pritchard attended the university, it was known as Western Reserve University. Western Reserve College was founded in 1826 in Hudson, Ohio about 30 miles south of Cleveland. It was named after the surrounding region known as the Western Reserve of Connecticut. The Medical Department was founded in 1843. In 1882, the college moved to its present location in Cleveland and became Western Reserve University. In 1877, philanthropist Leonard Case, Jr., started a school of applied science in Cleveland. The school—later (1947) named the Case Institute of Technology—moved to land adjacent to Western Reserve University in 1885. The two institutions partnered on various projects through the years. Their 1967 federation

pointed out that the military was about to take over the medical schools, and the students would be in the Army on active duty. He emphasized that he knew the Registrar and that he would try to get me an interview. He admitted that it was unlikely that she would be available but he would try.

From the outset the Registrar was not very friendly. I described my academic successes during Pharmacy School and saved as my "ace in the hole" my presumed excellent performance on the MCAT the previous December. I also pointed out my preparation for graduate school in Pharmacology. At this time, it was obvious that my interview was almost over. Standing behind her was the Dean who overheard the conversation. He urged the Registrar to look at my MCAT performance. They did and with little hesitation the Dean said, "Accept him!" She capitulated after we worked out a plan in which I would take one *bona fide* premedical course, namely embryology, and would have to get a B+ or better.

The freshman class had just begun so I would have to wait 8 months for the next class to start. The Dean spent the rest of the afternoon steering me over, around, and through obstacles. He recruited the help of a retired M.D. Army colonel who was organizing the Army Specialized Training Program (ASTP). The students admitted to medical school would be sworn in as second lieutenants on inactive duty. Until this was accomplished and Congress authorized funding of the program, however, the medical students would remain in civilian status, supporting themselves including paying all of their medical school expenses.

I was formally accepted as a freshman as soon as the current first-year students were promoted. This event was very important as it allowed me to be promptly sworn in as a second lieutenant. The Navy had expressed a desire to have me sworn in as a hospital corpsman or to allow for my induction into the Army as a private. My admittance to medical school and commission arrived in the mail just before my Naval swearing-in date. It directed me to go to the local

brought the institutions together under the name Case Western Reserve University. http://www.case.edu/stage/about/history.html

police station and be sworn in as a second lieutenant in the Army, then take a copy to the local draft board and await further orders – which I did. The Naval Recruiting Officer was upset to say the least, and the draft board was most confused but concluded that I was indeed exempt from the draft.

Since graduation from Pharmacy School in May 1942, I had worked as a pharmacist at another of the four local drug stores in Painesville. I continued to do this. The requirement by the Medical Registrar to satisfactorily complete a course in embryology was still in effect, and I did not wish to challenge it. The course during the summer ran from 1:00 p.m. until 5:00 p.m. The Pharmacist/Manager and I alternated hours to cover the store. I worked from morning opening at 8:00 a.m. until noon, then he covered from noon until 6:00 p.m. when I took over again until closing at 10:00 p.m. A Greyhound Bus picked me up in front of the drug store at noon in Painesville and dropped me off at the bus stop in front of the medical school in Cleveland at 1:00 p.m. At 5:00 p.m., I hopped on the same bus and rode back to the drug store. Fortunately, the drug store had a soda-sandwich bar that provided most of my nutritional needs. If my financial planning proved sound, I would accumulate enough money for the first year of medical school and with some help from my folks, it did!

I survived the long, hot summer and the cold winter. I remain forever grateful to my pharmacist colleague who supported my plan. Several years later, just after completing residency, I performed a cesarean section on his daughter-in-law who was visiting them while her husband, a Navy pilot, was off teaching Arthur Godfrey to fly a helicopter. I had gladly agreed to be available for any complications that might arise. The fetus was large, and she developed preeclampsia[13] and needed to be delivered promptly. For these two reasons, a cesarean section was performed. He expressed his gratitude for having participated in my training years earlier. Not only did we work together, he helped me get through embryology and into medical school. We both forgot that it was he who treated my finger after it was torn up by a bicycle wheel and chain more than 25 years before.

---

[13] Preeclampsia – the initial stage of a pregnancy complication often referred to as *toxemia of pregnancy*. See *eclampsia*; footnote 4.

MEDICAL SCHOOL 1943–1946

Medical school was condensed to train doctors more quickly to help meet the needs of the military. Torald Solmann, the Dean, was very protective of his students. (He is the one who reviewed my MCAT scores and insisted that I be accepted into medical school.) He retired because of his health and age during my second year of medical school. This prompted another remarkable change in my academic life. A new Chairman of Pharmacology, Arnold Welch from Washington University, was appointed. His training consisted of his graduating from pharmacy school, a Ph.D. in Pharmacology, and an M.D. degree. The department he inherited was for the most part mediocre. The Deanship drained off most of Solmann's energy leaving little for Pharmacology.

The new Chair was a fireball who hoped to make Pharmacology an important part of the war effort. He scrapped the entire archaic teaching program and installed one that emphasized therapeutics. For example, a variety of sulfonamides were shown to have antibacterial activity and were sorely needed for the wounded and/or infected troops. This is more like what I thought pharmacology would be.

Previously, competency in pharmacology was mostly determined by oral examinations. The new chair insisted on tough, frequent written examinations. Until this time, physiology and pathology commanded most all of the students' time. Rarely, if ever, did anyone fail pharmacology. With the new chairman, however, complacency became a thing of the past.

The consequence of failure could be as severe as dismissal from medical school and orders for immediate active duty. And, several in our class appeared to have failed the final examination! The Promotions Committee decided to raise all test scores across the board by a common value sufficient to bring everyone's grade to at least 75. Since I liked pharmacology very much, I spent much of my time studying it as opposed to pathology. When the extra increment was added to my original grade, it raised it to over 100. The Registrar refused to accept the new higher grade and apparently quarrelling ensued. Class standings were important for internship appointments. How this impasse was finally resolved I do not know. The last I heard, my final grade was only 100. During all the confusion, I was able to meet with Dr. Arnold Welch, the new Pharmacology Chair, and establish a friendship that influenced my later career.

ARMY SPECIALIZED TRAINING PROGRAM (ASTP)

Those of use who were privates in the Army were organized into a military company with commissioned and non-commissioned student officers. For reasons totally unclear – perhaps as a punishment – I was progressively promoted to Student Colonel. My commanding officer was a Captain who had been a junior high school principal in civilian life.

I was not too popular with some of my classmates during these times. I was cited by the new Chairman of Pharmacology as evidence that the examination could not have been too difficult. When I became Student Commander of the ASTP, I became the implement of the unpleasant orders issued by our commanding officer. I detested the job of Student Colonel. I had too much responsibility with negligible authority. A lesson learned!

There was one bright spot in this, however. At least once a month, all of the Army troops fell into formation and marched from the medical school across the main street in Cleveland for physical examinations, specifically for the presence of urethral discharge suggestive of gonorrhea. None was detected, and we all received the Good Conduct Medal!

Those marches to the health facility also introduced me to my wife-to-be.[14] The student nurses (she was a member of the Student

---

[14] Signe Allen was born in Willoughby, Ohio on November 28, 1923.

Nurse Cadet Corps) would come out onto the hospital balconies and cheer us on. I spotted her and she me, the Cadet Colonel. We later met at a Nu Sigma Nu fraternity function and began dating. During my third year (1945) of medical school, we decided to marry. The Army did not object to our marrying but Frances Payne Bolton School of Nursing[15] did. However, my position as Student Colonel of the ASTP unit and a favorable word from the former Dean of the medical school resulted in a waiver issued by the current Dean of the medical school.[16]

Pritchard Family Photo

Signe M. Allen – circa 1944

Student Nurse Cadet Corps
Frances Payne Bolton School of
Nursing

We continued to work hard. I received all A's from the time we married through graduation.

Luck played a role in this. Physical diagnosis was stressed. Initially, the students examined each other, and we started with the abdomen. We were forewarned that we would not find anything pathologic since we were examining healthy people.

However, I thought my partner's liver was enlarged and reported such. Our instructor laughed and said there are always a few students with a healthy imagination. But the liver enlargement was real, and my roommate was the first of nearly 30 students who ate the same lunch at our fraternity house and later developed hepatitis.

---

[15] The Frances Payne Bolton School of Nursing was part of Western Reserve University—now Case Western Reserve University. http://fpb.case.edu/

[16] Jack and Signe Pritchard were married in Kirtland, Ohio on March 9, 1945.

The instructor and I later became friends when he helped me with my research efforts. He translated my finding of the enlarged liver into a boost in my medicine grade.

My father had a long-standing inguinal hernia[17] which was aggravated by throwing switches at work on the B&O Railroad. He decided to have it repaired – not at University Hospital 30 miles away – but rather at the small community hospital in our hometown by the family doctor. He wanted to be able to look out the window and see familiar surroundings. I could not persuade him to go to our teaching hospital and be cared for by the surgical faculty.

I caught up with him after his surgery when he was waking up and obviously confused. As his sensorium cleared, it was apparent that he was pointing to the inguinal region and exclaiming loudly, "No! No! No!"

Guess what? The family practitioner had "repaired" the asymptomatic anatomically normal left side instead of the symptomatic, classic, large right inguinal hernia. Lots of confusion followed regarding the appropriate course of action. The physician wanted to operate again and hoped my father would consent. My father would be charged for none of this. Instead the physician would assume responsibility for all the medical costs. My father liked the doctor and could see how "anybody might make this mistake." The repair was made.

Almost immediately thereafter a flurry of bills from all the parties involved arrived at our house including bills from the physician for both procedures. My mother became furious and threatened a lawsuit. Acutely, the physician "took care" of all the charges from all the parties involved. Moreover, the physician urged my father to go to Florida and recuperate at the physician's expense. My dad forgave him, and they renewed their friendship. My father still thought that I could find a better occupation than the practice of medicine.

---

[17] Inguinal hernia – a protrusion of the lining of the abdominal cavity through a hole or weak area in the outer abdominal wall.

PHARMACOLOGY VERSUS AN OB/GYN INTERNSHIP

Until now, little firm thought had been given by most of us to our medical careers once the war was over. I was certainly confused. I finally narrowed it down to two routes: (1) Further training for a career in Pharmacology or (2) a career in Human Reproductive Biology, then called Obstetrics and Gynecology. The Pharmacology Chairman who tried to give me a grade greater than 100 assured me that a fellowship in pharmacology awaited me with his former mentors who had recently won the Nobel Prize.[18]

During my junior and senior years, I worked nights as a part-time extern at a general hospital with an active maternity service. The boyhood friend who had convinced my mother, and in turn me, that I should try for medical school was a resident physician there and was responsible for my being selected an extern. It was night work and Signe was a night nurse, so our work schedules conflicted minimally. This was my first real hospital experience. I really enjoyed it and was captivated by the many unanswered questions concerning human reproduction.

The Army insisted that we complete an internship after graduating. They promised a military internship if we did not find a civilian internship. The Chairman of the Medicine Department at Case Western Reserve University and his associates tempted me with serious offers of a career in internal medicine.

Reluctantly, I turned them down and applied for an internship in obstetrics and gynecology. I spent the next 15 months without salary in that role. I became disenchanted fairly quickly with Ob/Gyn as it was then practiced. Science was lacking to say the least. I wanted

---

[18] Joseph Erlanger and Herbert Spencer Gasser of Washington University, St. Louis, shared the 1944 Nobel Prize in Physiology or Medicine "for their discoveries relating to the highly differentiated functions of single nerve fibres." "The Nobel Prize in Physiology or Medicine 1944". Nobelprize.org. 9 Jun 2012.

http://www.nobelprize.org/nobel_prizes/medicine/laureates/1944/

out. An opportunity appeared to be at hand when the Army offered a number of ASTP trainees the opportunity to further postpone active military duty for another year. I decided to try to use the time to do a fellowship in Pharmacology; however, it was not that simple.

The military assumed that the year would be spent in residency training, not in graduate school. Nonetheless, after appreciable uncertainty, an Army friend of the Director of University Hospital of Cleveland was reached at the Pentagon and they guided my paperwork and finally approved me for a one-year fellowship in Pharmacology.

My fellowship stipend was $100 per month. How we were to raise the rest of the funds to survive was not clear. Some financial support from our families plus Signe's job as a nurse allowed us to exist. My father-in-law[19] was especially disgusted with trying to explain to acquaintances that even though I lived at a hospital and still wore a white suit, I was a genuine, licensed M.D.[20] He wished I would move on and prove it.

PHARMACOLOGY FELLOWSHIP

July 1, 1947 found me moving out of the Maternity Hospital 30 yards across the street to the Pharmacology Department in the medical school. Finding a parking place was an immediate problem and would continue to be for years to come. Space for laboratory efforts and a small office was not a problem. The very recently formed department was way understaffed. This also gave me the opportunity to teach medical and dental students as well as do research.

---

[19] Signe Pritchard's father was Max H. Allen.

[20] Jack Pritchard received his M.D. degree in March 1946 and his Ohio medical license in May 1946. Unlike today, interns and residents lived at the hospital where they were training. They were "in residence"—hence the name, *residents*.

The Chairman, Arnold Welch, was interested in folic acid metabolism, a recently identified vitamin especially essential for a variety of hematologic events as well as normal pregnancy. I obtained his collection of publications dealing with folic acid and began increasing my knowledge in this field.

I was intrigued by several of the published studies. According to some reports, folic acid was a fabulous compound, capable of even curing malignancy. I attempted to repeat the most dramatic of these studies. I could not confirm any of them. I submitted a report of my negative findings and it was promptly published.[21]

The Chairman and Head of the Hematology Department, Robert Heinle, had collaborated on studies in pigs in which a folic acid deficient diet was supplemented with an antifolic acid compound consisting of N-methyl folic acid. This compound had been shown to block folic acid action when given to rats and chicks but not rabbits. Some of the pigs, but not all, who received a synthetic N-methyl folic acid free diet developed anemia.

We finally determined the cause. Workmen in the animal unit were feeding lunch scraps to our pigs in spite of our signs "prohibiting" feeding the animals. It turned out that the amount of folic acid required for effective hematopoiesis[22] in pigs was much smaller than we and others had thought.[23] Time went fast and I learned a lot, including the fact that the printed word can be wrong.

---

[21] Pritchard JA. Failure of xanthopterin to influence hematopoiesis and growth in rats. *Proc Soc Exp Biol Med.* 1948 Nov;69(2):221-225.

[22] Hematopoiesis – formation and development of blood cells.

[23] Heinle RW, Welch AD, Pritchard JA. Essentiality of both the antipernicious anemia factor of liver and pteroylgutamic acid for hematopoiesis in swine. *J Lab Clin Med.* 1948 Dec;33(12):1647.

PHARMACOLOGY IN THE ARMY

Most all of us thought we would be released from the Army at the end of the year. After all, the military was downsizing. This was not the case for physicians who had been in the Army Specialized Training Program during our medical school days. I received notice that I would be ordered to active duty in June,[24] at the end of my year of deferment. I notified the Chairman of Pharmacology, who retraced some of the steps used to obtain my previous deferment. He succeeded in having the Army assign me to active duty at the Army Medical Department Research and Graduate School located on the Walter Reed Army Medical Center campus, but first I was ordered to Fort Sam Houston near San Antonio, Texas for a few weeks of basic training.

I had developed a sizeable inguinal hernia[17] (from "rasslin'" pigs to obtain blood), and I thought I might be separated from the military because of the hernia. On my re-entry physical examination, it was easily detected but only elicited the following recommendation: "When you get to your duty station you ought to get that fixed." The M.D. did issue an excuse for me from daily physical training which was most welcome in July, 1948 in Texas.

I arrived at the Pentagon on July 4th weekend to find no one around over the holiday. This gave me time to search for quarters for my wife and year-old son. I found a converted basement apartment which was livable except when the owner's quite obese son walked the floor over our heads.

No one at the Army Research and Graduate School seemed to know of my assignment there. I showed my orders around and somehow it was established that I was to be the Chief of the Pharmacology Section which personnel-wise consisted of – me. Then I met a Major who was career military whose permanent rank was Master Sergeant and, though he was scheduled for retirement soon, he took

---

[24] June, 1948.

me by the arm and invited me to meet the Commander, who was a Medical Corps Colonel also in the process of retiring. The Colonel thought I might work on the "emetine[25] problem." My escorting Major promptly stated that the emetine study had been completed. The Colonel replied that I probably had some interests of my own which I could undertake, so he showed me to an empty laboratory which he said would be all mine. He obtained a key for me to this sterile-looking laboratory, and a fabulous key it was as it opened nearly all the locks in the building.

I started to collect equipment to study the metabolism of the compound known initially as SN7618 and later as chloroquine for pre-vention of malaria. My Army Major colleague had been studying the interaction of two antimalarial compounds which were at times admin-istered together. I studied this only briefly but long enough to learn a few more laboratory techniques and confirm his observations.

I had been intrigued by the red cell's metabolic activity since it was normally anucleate.[26] I began a study of red cells and of their cholinesterase activity[27] and found that it varied inversely with red cell age. I submitted a manuscript that was accepted by a peer-review journal.[28] I learned a lot doing this study including how to borrow equipment without offending the apparent owner. Equipment was only requisitioned at glacial speed.

---

[25] Emetine – a drug produced from the ipeca root used in treatment of amoe-bic dysentery and to induce vomiting.

[26] Anucleate – lacking a cell nucleus.

[27] Cholinesterase activity – enzymatic action that splits acetylcholine into acetic acid and choline; activity occurs in blood serum as well as in the liver and pancreas.

[28] Pritchard JA. Erythrocyte age and cholinesterase activity. *Am J Physiol.* 1949 Jul;158(1):72-76.

NATIONAL INSTITUTES OF HEALTH

Through my former Chief of Pharmacology in Cleveland, I made friends with the Chief of the Nutrition Section at the National Institutes of Health (NIH) just up the road from Walter Reed Army Hospital and the Army Graduate School. He and his associates were working hard on the hematologic effects of folic acid. He proposed that I apply for a transfer from the Army to a position of comparable rank in the U.S. Public Health Service, of which the NIH was a research arm. I would then be assigned to the Nutrition Section at the National Institutes of Health.

I liked the idea. After discussion with my former Pharmacology Chief (and my wife of course), I set out to apply for this transfer. But wait – there was a fly in the ointment! I would have to undergo repair of my hernia in order to pass the required physical examination. No problem. Walter Reed had an abundance of surgeons looking for benign surgical cases for eligibility for the General Surgery Board Examination. An orthopedic surgeon, a colonel, was the surgeon assigned to me. It took forever and the spinal anesthesia wore off before he finished. The talk was to repeat the spinal. I had a near total spinal with the first injection and did not want to risk another. I instead pleaded for some morphine or Demerol and that they hurry up the procedure. (The hernia recurred a few years later.)

My convalescence was strange. Friends at the postgraduate school would drop by and act as if they were keeping something of importance from me. And, indeed they were. The Pentagon had somehow uncovered that I possessed an Obstetrical Specialist rating, and they were looking for one in Japan. I tried to point out that my training in Ob/Gyn consisted of only 15 months as an intern. My orders were set. I had two weeks in which to heal my hernia, move my wife and young son back to Ohio, and get to the port of embarkation in Seattle. After I protested, I was allowed an additional week. I sought out the individual who had originally paved the way for me to be assigned to Washington, D.C. He stated that the military was planning to start its own medical school and that young officers such as me would be strong candidates for senior faculty positions. (This actually did come to fruition several years later.)

I pointed out that it would be difficult for me to cover obstetrics full-time in Japan but I would not mind if my wife and infant son could accompany me. He did find out that coordinated overseas travel had been established recently for all medical doctors and their immediate dependents. Unfortunately, I got to be the last medical officer who would not receive coordinated travel thanks to the Transportation Corps. Finally, I told him that I felt unqualified to practice solo with my limited clinical training. What about a laboratory position? He said that a good friend, the Chief of Laboratories for the Far East Command, was visiting in Washington, D.C. and he would contact him on my behalf. I never heard from the Pentagon Personnel Officer or the Far East Command Laboratory Officer.

OVERSEAS

I arrived in Seattle and reported as ordered only to languish there for two weeks! I pointed out that I was needed in Japan. This was the real Army, however, and "everybody was needed somewhere." We just milled around doing nothing but dodge raindrops. I met an interesting but depressed fellow M.D. who was returning from Tokyo. His job for one-plus years was to ensure that Tojo remained alive until "hanged by the neck until dead" – which he did. Several M.D.s gave me their uniforms which was a good thing because my "hold" luggage had been lost between Seattle and Yokohama.

Finally, we departed by ship for Yokohama as a band stood at the end of the dock playing "On a Slow Boat to China." It was not a pleasant trip. It appeared that all my officer shipmates had their dependents with them. We arrived in Yokohama one typhoon later. As we entered Tokyo Bay with beautiful Mount Fuji in the background, we received the announcement that some of us might be sent to evacuate Americans and other friendly countrymen from Shanghai which was falling to the Chinese Communists at that time.

Pritchard Family Photo
Capt. Jack A. Pritchard, M.D.
Chief of Ob/Gyn, Sendai, Japan
Army of the United States
1948–1950

After we docked in Yokohama, we waited for another week to be taken by troop train to Sendai. There were two train commanders – one M.D. (me) and one infantry officer – responsible for several hundred troops that had been sworn in the U.S. and immediately shipped to Japan for all of their basic training.

I pointed out to the infantry officer that regulations protected medical officers from such duty. (I am not sure this was true). He took all the paperwork, placed a detail in charge of our food (C rations that were stolen in the course of our train trip), and acted at least like he enjoyed his duties. Sendai was a 200+ mile overnight trip.

An ambulance from the hospital was waiting for me at 8:00 a.m. when we arrived at the Sendai rail station. There was an obstetrical problem! An officer's wife was late in pregnancy, not in labor but looked large. Should she be evacuated to Tokyo in case she needed a cesarean? Though I had not seen a pregnant woman as a patient since graduating from medical school more than three years before, I examined the woman and concluded that we did not need to evacuate her. She delivered spontaneously, and mother and baby (fortunately) did well.

I thought I remembered how to do a cesarean section satisfactorily and performed one a week or so later. The hospital commander was furious since I had done it while he was away. "It could have waited until I returned," he exclaimed. We did it for fetal distress, I told him, which I presumed required prompt intervention.

Another patient, a recently married Army nurse, had been admitted for threatened abortion; and when her symptoms abated, she was let out on a pass. She was told to return if her symptoms reappeared, which they did, and now she became my patient. I was quite concerned that she might have an ectopic pregnancy' and informed the Commander that she would need surgery before it ruptured. He was incensed. I emphasized that it could rupture at any time, causing hemorrhagic shock and even death if surgery and blood transfusions were delayed. His plan was to send her to Tokyo General Hospital. I pointed out that Tokyo General was 16 hours away, and she might not tolerate such a delay, especially if there was hemorrhage. He countered that we would send a nurse with a unit of blood which would safeguard the patient if there was a rupture on the way. Well, it did rupture and though the patient did suffer blood loss, she recovered.

A medical library was essentially absent in Japan. Immediately upon arrival I asked Signe to send me my *Williams Textbook of Obstetrics*[29] from my medical school days, which she did along with some popcorn and a popcorn popper.

Obstetric business was slow. During the nearly one year that I spent in Sendai, there were only three other major obstetric cases. The first was delivery of Japanese Ambassador Karusu's daughter. She was married to a first lieutenant West Point graduate stationed near our hospital. Her pelvis was simply too small for the half-caucasian fetus. With a ban on cesarean section in place, I resorted to a difficult forceps delivery.

Of interest, Karusu was the special envoy sent to the White House allegedly to assure our State Department that Japan was not about to wage war against the U.S. At the same time, Japanese planes and warships were closing in on Pearl Harbor. Karusu's cau-

---

[29] The 9th edition was the first to have this title. Authored by Henricus J. Stander, it was published by Appleton-Century-Crofts in 1945. Before his death in 1948, Stander authored the 7th, 8th, and 9th editions of John Whitridge Williams' *Obstetrics*. Williams initially published the textbook in 1903 and was responsible for its first six editions; the last of which was published in 1930. Stander had been a protégé of Williams at Johns Hopkins and took over as author/editor after Williams died following minor surgery on October 21, 1931.

casian wife (the baby's grandmother) was a U.S. citizen by birth but had become a Japanese citizen before the war.

The second was a case of placental abruption[30] in which the mother developed sudden severe abdominal pain, a tetanic uterus,[31] and appreciable vaginal bleeding late in pregnancy. No fetal heart sounds were heard. As I had written a paper on placental abruption in my senior year of medical school, the diagnosis seemed obvious. I urged mobilization of a surgical team to perform a cesarean section and to transfuse fresh donor blood to combat hemorrhagic shock. The Commandant was enraged. While I was preparing for an immediate cesarean section to save a woman's life, he was entertaining the U.S. Army Deputy Surgeon General and his team from the Pentagon in the Officers Club one floor above. He urged me to simply pack the uterus! They were at the 172nd Station Hospital trying to recruit physicians for the regular Army – a sales pitch I had been subjected to months before at Walter Reed Hospital. Needless to say, we did not pack the uterus. Rather, we went ahead with the cesarean section and the woman's postoperative convalescence was uncomplicated.

The day before Christmas a call came in to the Commander's office with a plea for help from the 161st Station Hospital 150 miles north of us. A woman had delivered a baby without difficulty but the placenta remained adherent to the uterus. The physician handling the case said he was not trained to handle this emergency and would not be responsible for her further care. The Commander wanted me to do something. My conversation with the nurse who was with the patient confirmed what I had already been told. I stated that manual removal of the placenta was indicated, if it could be performed. Otherwise, continuous vigorous treatment for hemorrhage shock and a hysterectomy would be necessary. No one there, however, was capable of providing such treatment.

The Commanding General of the Seventh Infantry Division

---

[30] Placental abruption – when the placenta detaches from the uterine wall before the baby is born; also called *placenta abruptio*.

[31] Tetanic uterus – state of constant contraction without relaxation, producing constant twitching.

headquartered near us had his own plane and pilot. (Interestingly, he had graduated from medical school before the war and had transferred to the Infantry Division.) His pilot offered to fly me to a landing strip near the 161st Hospital. I felt obligated to go even though my obstetric training was limited, the terrain deplorable, and the weather terrible. We flew along the backbone of the mountain range that runs north and south on the island of Honshu to Hachinoe. We eventually found the landing strip near the hospital even though there was little daylight the day before Christmas in northern Japan. A jeep was waiting for us and we were soon at the hospital. I had urged them to quickly find more type O blood donors and pump blood, and they had started doing this. The patient was arousable but far from alert. I put on gloves and explored the uterine cavity. I manually developed a cleavage plane between the uterine wall and placenta. The placenta separated completely and was lifted out of the intact uterus, which then contracted firmly. This compressed the vessels in the uterine implantation site, arresting the bleeding. The patient soon awakened.

It was Christmas Eve and word spread throughout the base that a big healthy baby had been born. When details of the complications became known, all the pilots thanked me, and one insisted on flying me back to Sendai. I refused, saying that I would ride the overnight train, "The Dixie Limited," which would drop me off in Sendai on its way to Tokyo. I told them the weather scared me but they said they flew in it all the time. I now realized why as Laboratory Officer I was handling so many crash bags from their jet base. Finally, they had a nightcap and the "volunteers" dispersed.

Christmas 1949 was a sad day. My presents consisted only of a Red Cross Emergency Care package and a pipe that never stopped burning my tongue. I had insisted that the families not send me anything because rumor had it that the 38 or so physicians in my category (Army of United States, rather than the United States Army) would be separated before Christmas because Congress had allowed our funding to expire. As soon as MacArthur's Far East Command learned of this, separation from the Army of the United States stopped! Funds came from somewhere to pay our salaries.

I heard from the Chairman of Pharmacology occasionally. He had accepted the Chair at Yale and was holding a position for me. Another move? My family needed someplace to call home that was more than just a mailing address. Also, my exposure again to clinical obstetrics rekindled my enthusiasm, which was further fanned by a letter from the Acting Chairman at Cleveland University Hospital. He pointed out that it was almost certain that a young academician, well trained in clinical and laboratory reproductive medicine from Johns Hopkins Medical School would soon be appointed full-time chairman at Cleveland Maternity. The young academician expressed his desire to have someone with my background join him in Cleveland. I accepted even though my position was ill defined. What and when do I tell the Chairman of Pharmacology now at Yale?

Surprisingly, in March 1950 I received orders to return to the U.S. for separation, if my hospital commander approved – which he did!

GOING HOME

My travel back to the States was non-commodious to say the least on a very old troop ship, the *U.S.A.T. Haase*. We very slowly crossed the Pacific while the GIs chipped rust and painted the hull trying to clean her up before transferring her from the Army Transportation Corps to the U.S. Navy. The same day I sailed, another medical officer left for the United States on a sleek, fast transport, the *Morton*. Why not me? Bad luck? Not really as you will see later.

We docked in San Francisco. It was a beautiful sight watching the sun come up behind the Golden Gate Bridge! I was in search of transportation to Pittsburgh, California, about 50 miles inland where – according to the orders issued in Tokyo – I was supposed to be separated from the Army. I spotted a young transportation officer and asked him if he might be driving to Pittsburgh, the Army Replacement Depot. He said, "Sure, hop in." He dropped me off at the Separation

Station. I went in and a sergeant immediately started the process of getting me out of the Army. It was very simple. Not even a physical examination even though I had been hospitalized for the hernia repair during my time on active duty. He commented that rumor had it that some doctors from the Orient were not to be separated until they had completed a full two years of service. That would have meant I had 3 more months in the military. I told him it must have just been a rumor; I was in a different group! (I wanted out now – not three months from now!) He handed me my separation papers and directed me to the finance office where I was paid off and told goodbye.

The night before I had purchased tickets on a charter flight to Cleveland. I was still in uniform even though the war had ended some years before.[32] (We were not allowed to wear civilian clothes in the Far East.) Between storms and other changes in flight "non"-schedules, we moved west to east most of the time across the country to reach Cleveland where my wife and young son awaited me.

HAPPY FAMILY REUNION

Back in Ohio, my wife was terrified by my driving. I had been driving on the "wrong" side of the road for nearly a year in Japan and unconsciously continued to do so in the United States. When I went to the University Maternity Hospital, MacDonald House, in 1950 to begin my reorientation as an assistant resident in Ob/Gyn, I was shocked to find that individuals who had been medical students when I was previously there were now junior faculty or senior residents. The experience was a sad one but I honored my houseofficer's contract. I was tempted to beg forgiveness one more time of the Chairman of Pharmacology at Yale.

---

[32] World War II ended five years earlier in 1945.

KOREAN WAR

All of a sudden the world was again topsy-turvy. North Korea had invaded South Korea and the Korean War was on.[33] Physicians were being mobilized from most every nook and cranny to serve in the military. Those who trained under the Navy V-12 program during World War II and had never been required to pay back any time had to report immediately. Those trained by the Army Specialized Training Program were vulnerable if they had served on active duty for less than 21 months. I had served 21 months and 5 days. A reprieve at least for the moment. Had I been sent home from Japan on the newer and faster troop transport instead of that old rust bucket, the U.S.A.T. Haase, I would have been called back to active duty. Thank the Lord for rusty ships!

Several of my fellow residents were promptly ordered to active duty. This hampered the care of our patients and those of us who were left all worked 36-hour shifts with only 12 hours between. We walked around like zombies and got no relief. The completion of a Ph.D. in Pharmacology again looked tempting. Arnold Welch, now the Chairman at Yale, went so far as to arrange with the Chairman of Ob/Gyn at Yale, Lee Buxten, for me to have a formal joint appointment in both departments. It was tempting but, after visiting New Haven, I turned it down. The new Chairman of Ob/Gyn from Johns Hopkins, Gilbert Vosburgh, was now on board at Cleveland Maternity.

A NEW CHAIRMAN (NUMBER 5)

Dr. Vosburgh in 1950 brought with him from Baltimore a resident who also had some fellowship training. He said he had plans for both of us in academic Ob/Gyn.

---

[33] The Korean War lasted from 25 June 1950 until 27 July 1953.

The workload did not get any easier. The two of us got no special favors on the clinical side. To qualify for certification as a specialist in Ob/Gyn, you had to complete three years of residency training. The resident from Johns Hopkins left the program very soon after becoming board eligible.

Dr. Vosburgh set about cleaning out potentially dangerous procedures that continued to be applied long after the "revered founder" of our department, Dr. Arthur Bill, had retired. A home-delivery service still prevailed. If the pregnant woman had ever been seen in one of the outpatient clinics and she was judged to have no complications, she was told that when she experienced labor pains 5 minutes apart to call back and the (student) doctors would be on their way. In the meantime, boil water and collect newspapers for "drapes." A resident physician would then come to the house and supervise a "normal spontaneous delivery."

If the woman had been seen antepartum and the pregnancy was judged likely to be complicated, she was directed to go to the University Hospital Emergency Suite where a decision would be made to admit or observe her. She might still be sent home or to Cleveland City Hospital if no other prenatal care had been provided. All regulations were loosely applied. Most women were to stay home and deliveries often ended up resembling a Chinese fire drill. The senior medical students liked dashing around town in scrub suits carrying their black delivery bags and having the neighbors direct them to the house where the baby was to be born. I knew of no maternal deaths but one resident did drown when he made a wrong turn into the Cuyahoga River.

I was the last resident "supervisor" on the last home delivery at midnight, December 31, 1952. The house was in the midst of the New York Central Railroad Roundhouse. As all of the locomotives blared their horns and whistles to welcome in the New Year, the sound of a baby crying lustily could be heard. It was the end of an era.

Hospital deliveries were much different from the home deliver-

ies. The woman typically arrived at the hospital having had a few labor pains. She was placed on a combination labor-delivery bed.
Then she was started on analgesia consisting of scopolamine and
morphine or Demerol, and later ether by cone inhalation. The woman
was amnesic[34] and /or anesthetized.

Two medical students would then rotate this limp patient 90
degrees, placing her legs and lower thighs off the edge of the special
labor-delivery bed. Each student would then grasp a leg, flexing it at
the knee and hip, and sit down on the edge of the bed. Subsequently,
the patient was draped from chest to toe after the vagina and perito-
neum were vigorously scrubbed. The physician would now scrub,
gown, and glove, and ask the nurse assistant to check the condition of
the cervix. He would then pronounce that delivery was imminent.

Although it was taught that delivery required a completely dilated cervix and an engaged fetal head,[35] these criteria were often
waived. Instead, the cervix would be dilated manually until it could be
slipped over the fetal head and the head either pushed through the
vagina or pulled out with forceps or, more likely, both. Forceps were
the rule for all deliveries. The housestaff were directed to mimic
closely the private practitioners. At delivery, the infant was typically
depressed[36] and the leg-holders got an upside down view of a "delivery."

Dr. Vosburgh, the new chairman, was aghast at what he wit-
nessed and wanted to change a lot of things, but he did not know how
to assume command. Mostly confusion prevailed. Unfortunately, he
was not a skilled leader and the private practitioners either ignored
him or went to the hospital administrator with their complaints and
recommendations. The administrators were in a bind. They needed
patient revenue, and the private practitioners were the obstetricians

---

[34] Amnesic – state of partial or total loss of memory.

[35] Engaged fetal head – when the baby's head has entered the upper opening of the birth canal in the mother's pelvis.

[36] Depressed infant – one whose appearance is pale and whose functions
are slower than normal, *e.g.*, slow heart rate, not breathing well; medically referred to as an infant with a low apgar score.

for most of the Cleveland "elite" and sympathetic to their complaints. Some private obstetricians decided to boycott the University Hospitals by taking their patients elsewhere and more threatened to do so.

Then a strange event occurred. The new chairman was drafted even though he was known to have significant heart disease and had been turned down repeatedly for active duty during World War II. Vosburgh was "relieved" of his command and "Mo" Black, the old faithful volunteer temporary chairman, took over one more time. He, in turn, allowed me lots of leeway in patient management and on research projects. At this point I had now worked under the following Ob/Gyn Chairmen: Bill, Black, Vosburg, and Black again. A search committee was formed to find a replacement for the chairman recently from Johns Hopkins. Pretty soon I would be working under Chairman Number Five.

SOME EARLY INITIAL STUDIES OF HEMATOLOGIC CHANGES IN PREECLAMPSIA-ECLAMPSIA[4] – AND ANOTHER NEW CHAIRMAN

An apparently well-qualified individual, Allan Barnes from the Ohio State School of Medicine, seemed to be a good choice for the chair. He was Chair at Ohio State and known widely for his speaking ability. It was also known that he was unhappy at Ohio State when the Dean, against the wishes of Dr. Barnes, appointed to full professor, Richard Melling, an older but only very recently and minimally-trained individual.

A novel situation gradually evolved. The Chairman at Ohio State became the Chairman at Case Western Reserve, and the recently appointed professor at Ohio State became the new Chairman at Ohio State. These arrangements, however, were not completely satisfactory. Barnes was unhappy in Cleveland; and when offered the Chair at Johns Hopkins, he accepted. The Chairman of Ob/Gyn at Ohio State then became the Dean of the Medical School at Ohio State.

During this time I supervised the clinic obstetric service and was also available for consultation on private patients. Dr. Barnes, the new chairman, insisted I stay on. I was appointed a fellow as well as Chief Resident and with that received a sizeable salary boost. I was given a small but adequate laboratory and was free to essentially study whatever I wished as long as patient care was not neglected. At last, life was more satisfactory.

PREECLAMPSIA–ECLAMPSIA

I had long been interested in preeclampsia-eclampsia, then also referred to as toxemia of pregnancy. Management of women with this malady and their fetuses bordered on schizophrenia. I became directly involved in their clinical treatment using the variety of agents popular at that time. One day blood I had personally drawn for various laboratory studies from a woman with apparent eclampsia had grossly hemolysed. I drew more blood but the hemolysis[37] persisted. It was definitely not due to faulty technique. Life was becoming quite exciting!

I sought the help of two young colleagues, Oscar Ratnoff and Russell Weisman, hematologists in the Department of Medicine. We went to work and found a variety of changes known to be associated with hemolysis including severe thrombocytopenia.[38] Was this a new entity? Unfortunately, we procrastinated too long, afraid of hemorrhage if she was delivered by cesarean section. The patient developed a massive cerebral hemorrhage and died. In retrospect, we had failed to control her severe hypertension! Soon thereafter, we identified a second case of apparent eclampsia with hemolysis and severe

---

[37] Hemolysis – a condition in which red cells break open releasing hemoglobin into the surrounding plasma.

[38] Thrombocytopenia – a condition where the number of blood platelets (blood cells involved in clotting) are abnormally low.

thrombocytopenia.   Although hemodialysis[39] was attempted, the woman developed renal failure and died of hypokalemia.[40] Within a short period of time a third similar case was seen. This time, we promptly delivered liveborn twins by cesarean section. The mother very soon became normal, and she and her twins thrived.

I still do not know why rarely some women who develop apparent eclampsia behave in this way. Subsequent observations have established that prompt delivery is important for a favorable outcome with this severe pregnancy complication. Labeling it the "HELLP syndrome"[41] has not served to shed much light on its pathogenesis. "Fractured" red cells were prominent and probably caused the hemoglobinemia.[42] But what caused the traumatized red cells?

We promptly prepared a manuscript for publication and submitted it to the prestigious *New England Journal of Medicine*. It was turned down. Shortly thereafter, the Chairman of Obstetrics at Harvard, Dr. Duncan Reid, came to Cleveland to speak to the Cleveland Obstetric Society. His sponsor had an emergency, and I was called upon to "entertain" the visiting chairman. As we started out, my emergency pager went off – a private patient with eclampsia!

I had previously drawn up a protocol for treating eclampsia, and I was pleased to see it being implemented by a nurse as we arrived at the patient's bedside. I administered 4 grams of magnesium sulfate slowly by intravenous injection, followed promptly by 5 grams intramuscularly in each buttock. She soon stopped convulsing and not long afterwards was arousable. Hydralazine was given intravenously in divided doses to lower the diastolic blood pressure to below 110 millimeters of mercury (mm Hg). The visiting chairman from Bos-

---

[39] Hemodialysis – mechanically cleansing the blood outside the body to remove substances that would normally be removed by the kidney.

[40] Hypokalemia – a condition where the level of potassium in the blood serum is very low, adversely affecting muscles like the heart.

[41] HELLP – an acronym for the following characteristics of eclampsia: Hemolysis, Elevated Liver enzymes, Low Platelets.

[42] Hemoglobinemia – excessive hemoglobin (red blood cells) in blood plasma.

ton was most favorably impressed. He said he could not remember when he had last seen a case of eclampsia.

A little later the subject of the hematologic changes associated with eclampsia came up. I started to mention our unusual cases, and he said he was familiar with them as he had reviewed the manuscript we had submitted to the *New England Journal of Medicine*. "When is it due out?" he asked.

I told him the paper had been rejected and went to retrieve a copy of the letter and the manuscript. He looked them over and emphasized that a serious error had been made. He retired to an empty office and called the editor at the *New England Journal of Medicine*. When he came out, he assured me that the article was now accepted and would be published very soon, which it was.[43] He said he had reviewed it and been favorably impressed by it. He then gave it to another member of his department to review never thinking that it would be flatly turned down by the second reviewer. It turned out that there may have been some preexisting hard feelings between one of my coauthors and the second reviewer.

MAGNESIUM SULFATE ($MgSO_4 \cdot 7H_2O$)

I continued the studies of eclampsia and especially the use of magnesium sulfate in its treatment. A number of misconceptions were uncovered and included the following: Even though magnesium sulfate had long been given presumably to lower blood pressure in a variety of circumstances, it did so only transiently or not at all in hypertensive adults and children. When magnesium sulfate was rapidly injected intravenously, the blood pressure fell but only during the time that intense vasodilation took place. It then rose back up to or near

---

[43] Pritchard JA, Weisman R Jr., Ratnoff OD, Vosburgh GJ. Intravascular hemolysis, thrombocytopenia and other hematologic abnormalities associated with severe toxemia of pregnancy. *N Engl J Med.* 1954 Jan 21; 250(3):89-98.

preinjection levels. (I remain indebted to my colleagues in Internal Medicine and Pediatrics who allowed me to do this simple study in non-obstetric hypertensive subjects.)

It was long believed, by some neurologists at least, that magnesium sulfate was not an anticonvulsant. Why? Because it did not seem to cross the blood-brain barrier. We demonstrated repeatedly that magnesium sulfate most often promptly arrested convulsions in eclamptic women. This argument has raged for years, especially between one neurologist, James Donaldson, and myself. He considered the use of magnesium sulfate to be malpractice and recommended several other agents. When I last contacted him, he had never treated a case of eclampsia. We had published our results using primarily magnesium sulfate in 254 consecutive cases of eclampsia without a single death. Yet in his neurology textbook, he devotes a great deal of space to his recommended treatment of eclampsia with no regard for our published results.

It was reported recently that contractions *in vitro* of myometrial strips[44] was impaired by parenteral[45] magnesium sulfate. I observed that women with severe placental abruption[30] were prone to deliver soon after injection. We concluded tentatively that the uterus relaxed allowing the fetus and placenta to be expelled. What we did not appreciate was that this mechanism was no different from that in cases not receiving magnesium sulfate. In cases of severe placental abruption with spontaneous labor, the cervix typically did little in the way of dilatation until completely effaced[46] when the fetus then rapidly delivered.

We obtained a multichannel tokodynamometer which we used to record the pattern of uterine contractions during labor with and without administering magnesium sulfate. There was overall essentially no change in frequency, duration or maximum intensity of the

---

[44] Myometrial strips – strips of tissue taken from the middle layer of the uterine wall (myometrium) and studied in the laboratory (*in vitro*).

[45] Parenteral – administration by subcutaneous or intramuscular injection rather than through the alimentary canal.

[46] Effaced – thinned and stretched prior to delivery.

contractions. In some instances, the uterine contraction pattern disappeared for a few minutes only to reappear in its original form 8 to 12 minutes later. Since then many reports have been published claiming that magnesium sulfate is effective in arresting unwanted labor. My experience has been that, if it did so, it did so poorly. The argument for its use in these instances seems to be "We did not have anything better!"

Important toxicologic features of magnesium sulfate were confirmed, including that loss of knee jerk was a clinical sign of significant toxicity, and respiratory depression was evidence of overdose and the need for prompt treatment. The presence of a knee jerk ruled out dangerous toxicity.

Somehow during all the turmoil, I was able to find time with the aid of co-authors to prepare three manuscripts: one dealing with the clinical and laboratory observations of the woman with a hematologic variant of eclampsia, which was published in the *New England Journal of Medicine*;[47] another was an extensive study of magnesium metabolism used in the treatment of preeclampsia-eclampsia which was published in *Surgery, Gynecology and Obstetrics*,[48] and the third was a study of the effects of posture on renal function late in pregnancy published in the *Journal of Clinical Investigation*.[49] Importantly, the protocol for the treatment of eclampsia was established and became one that proved subsequently in Dallas to be highly effective in preventing maternal mortality from this serious malady.

In July 1954, I was freed from bondage as Chief Resident and Fellow and appointed Assistant Professor of Ob/Gyn at Case Western Reserve School of Medicine. It was a long time coming, from March

---

[47] Ratnoff OD, Pritchard JA,. Colopy JE. Hemorrhagic states during pregnancy. *N Engl J Med.* 1955 Jul 14;253(2):63-69; continued in *N Engl J Med.* 1955 Jul 21;253(3):97-102

[48] Pritchard JA. The use of the magnesium ion in the management of eclamptogenic toxemias. *Surg Gynecol Obstet.* 1955 Feb;100 (2): 131-140.

[49] Pritchard JA, Barnes AC, Bright RH. The effect of the supine position on renal function in the near-term pregnant woman. *J Clin Invest.* 1955 Jun;34 (6):777-781.

1946 to July 1954.[50]

WE MOVE TO DALLAS – 1955

In March 1955, I received a call from the University of Texas Southwestern Medical School in Dallas, Texas stating that a committee had been formed to search for a Chairman of Obstetrics and Gynecology and that my name had been suggested. Ernest Muirhead, Chairman of the Committee, painted an impressive picture. I politely refused but we talked further discussing our common interests and the potential that the school offered. Later, a call from A.J. Gill, Dean of Southwestern Medical School, encouraged me to think some more about the job. He had somehow found out that a close Army friend of mine from the 172nd Hospital in Sendai, Japan and a graduate of Southwestern, Robert Bone,[51] was now in practice 60 miles from Dallas and that he and his wife wanted to renew acquaintances.

We were soon on our way to Dallas. We were not quite prepared for the decrepit buildings which housed the clinical science departments – the "shacks" as they were called. There was a new Basic Science Building adjacent to the new Parkland Memorial Hospital and the promise of a new Clinical Science Building.

---

[50] During his residency in Ob/Gyn (July 1950–June 1954), Dr. Pritchard also published the following articles—

Pritchard JA. A simplied method for estimating sodium in urine and in fluid from the gastrointestinal tract. *Am J Clin Pathol.* 1953 Sep;23(9):942-945.

Pritchard JA. Coarctation of the aorta and pregnancy. *Obstet Gynecol Surv.* 1953;8(6):775-791.

Pritchard JA. Ratnoff OD, Weisman R Jr. Hemostatic defects and increased red cell destruction in pre-eclampsia and eclampsia. *Obstet Gynecol.* 1954 Aug;4(2):159-164.

Ratnoff OD, Colopy JE, Pritchard JA. The blood-clotting mechanism during normal parturition. *J Lab Clin Med.* 1954 Sep;44 (3):408-415.

[51] Robert Bone graduated from Southwestern Medical School in the class of 1946—the last class to graduate under the ASTP program.

Southwestern Medical College – Prefabricated plywood buildings—circa 1955.

From Dallas Medical Images, UT Southwestern Collection (uts_00025). Creator—Unknown.

The Chairman of the Search Committee had been negotiating with Jack Leonards, a Professor of Biochemistry at Case Western Reserve, over an artificial kidney built by Leonards. Leonards and I had done some of the magnesium studies together. He apparently gave a flattering description of my qualifications. He supposedly said that he would let me do a hysterectomy on his wife – presumably this qualified me for the Gyn part of the Ob/Gyn departmental title.

The Committee reviewed my publications and current research efforts and were impressed. Dean Gill was quite conservative. He was new at his job and had inherited some serious problems, including a brawl between the heads of Radiology and Ob/Gyn over who would treat cancer of the cervix. Had I known the intensity of the battle between the radiologist, Ralph Clayton, and William Mengert, the Chairman of Ob/Gyn, and how it nearly consumed the town/gown relationships, I probably would have declined the position.

Southwestern Medical College Basic Science Hall—circa 1955.
The Basic Science Hall—dedicated January 29, 1955—was renamed in honor of Edward H. Cary, M.D., on October 7, 1960. The new Parkland Memorial Hospital, which opened in 1954, is in the background on the left.

From Dallas Medical Images, UT Southwestern Collection (uts_00008). Creator— Unknown.

Each Wednesday afternoon there was a presentation of general scientific interest. A local faculty member was bumped, and I was given the hour for a presentation of my choice. I had been going over serial observations I recently had made on the spontaneous disruption of the maternal coagulation mechanism when a fetus died and remained *in utero*. The presentation was well received, especially by the Chairman of the Search Committee, whose research interests as the Chairman of Pathology were heavily weighted toward hematology. They offered me the job.

My wife was favorably impressed with Dallas and the potential for a decent living. We both agreed I should take the job in spite of my youth. I accepted the position and all of the Search Committee members remained quite supportive.

The Dean of Case Western Reserve, Joseph Wearn, learned I had gone to look at the job in Dallas and arranged a meeting with me post-haste. Even though I had been on and off campus for 12 years, this was the first time I had ever spoken with him. I had only seen him from a distance a few times. What a charmer! He was Ivy League through and through. He emphasized that if I stayed in Cleveland and continued to be productive I would surely be offered a position at a major medical school such as Harvard or Yale. I thanked him. I had already received offers from both of those schools and had turned them down.

Allan Barnes, Chairman of Ob/Gyn and still my boss in Cleveland, wanted to know if Southwestern had offered me the Chair and what I was going to do. I told him that I thought I would stay in my Assistant Professor position. He surprised me by stating that if I stayed in Cleveland, I would be Chief at Cleveland City (Maternity) Hospital. And so I said "goodbye" to Case Western Reserve Medical School.

We had no money with which to move to Dallas. Dean Gill offered us some of his precious Southwestern Medical School Funds which provided for emergencies not covered by the University of Texas appropriations. We arrived with our three boys,[52] aged 7, 4 and 18 months during one of the hottest, driest summers on record. Our boys thought it would be like the cowboy movies. On deplaning at Love Field, one of them exclaimed, "This is just as hot as Cleveland!"

When I arrived in Dallas, the animosity between the radiologists and the Ob/Gyn practitioners had escalated. My view was that advanced invasive cervical cancer was best treated by irradiation. Early invasive cancer could be treated either by irradiation or surgery. I had expressed my views to the Search Committee. I had also urged

---

[52] The Pritchards' sons are Jack Allen (1947), David George (1951), and Allen Jeffrey (1954).

the Committee to consider hiring a well-trained radiologist and radio-therapist that I knew at Case Western Reserve School of Medicine, Frederick Bonte. Yes, we had worked together. Yes, we were compatible. Fred became Chairman of Radiology, and I remained Chairman of Obstetrics & Gynecology.

Pritchard Family Photo

Jack A. Pritchard, M.D.—1955

Professor and Chairman
Department of Obstetrics and
Gynecology

Several of the Ob/Gyn community senior practitioners desired faculty appointments with senior rank, namely Clinical Professor, especially if they were to work without remuneration in the department. A few threatened further boycott of the department if promotions to Clinical Professor were made only for those few who constituted a vocal minority.

One of the minority in particular claimed to have extraordinary clinical skills as well as remarkable teaching capabilities. He made sure that his mostly wealthy, influential patients knew of these alleged special talents. Threats circulated that if he alone were promoted, most of the other senior clinical staff would have nothing to do with the department.

A justifiable but simple solution was found: Appoint all as Clinical Professors of Obstetrics & Gynecology with a letter of acceptance to be signed if they still wished to be "promoted." Two who had complained the loudest did not even bother to sign the letter and mail it to the Office of the Dean. The majority, however, did and subsequently provided worthwhile instruction for our medical students, interns, and residents.

After working out a few other mild conflicts I accepted the job as Chairman of Obstetrics & Gynecology at the University of Texas Southwestern Medical School and Chief of Ob/Gyn at Parkland Memorial Hospital. At age 33, I was the youngest Chairman of Obstetrics & Gynecology in the United States. There were members of the housestaff that were older than me!

What else went with this job? Not much except an enormous responsibility for 4,000+ deliveries annually that were rising rapidly, the training of nearly 200 medical students annually, and most importantly, the training of competent specialists in obstetrics and gynecology. The department budget was $57,000 a year. The salary of the Chairman was $15,000. The faculty members at the medical school were not allowed to have private practice.

There was a jewel of a secretary, Juanita Epperson,[53] who somehow held the department together. The one full-time Associate Professor, Stewart Fish,[54] announced as I arrived that he was about to go to sea as a cruise doctor. There was a handyman, Robert,[55] who tried to keep the shacks together and turned out to be competent in handling small animals. In fact, his anesthesia mortality rate in rats was lower than that of a full-time anesthesiologist. By the way, the shacks were more than a mile away from the new hospital.

---

[53] Juanita Epperson joined the department February 1, 1947, retired August 31, 1983, and came back part time from September 2, 1983 through January 31, 1985—a total of 38 years of service.

[54] Stewart Fish was acting chair July 1 through August 31, 1955.

[55] The handyman was Robert Wright. He and Juanita Epperson are listed on the 1955–1956 state budget.

OBSTETRICS AND GYNECOLOGY

Jack A. Pritchard, Chairman

	1953-54	1954-55	1955-56
Professor Jack A. Pritchard	$ . . .	$ . . .	$10,600(a)
(Professor)	10,600	10,600	. . .
Associate Professor	. . .	. . .	8,500 (-2,000)=
Assistant Professor Stewart Fish	6,000	6,000(b)	7,400(b).
(Assistant Professor)	7,000	7,000	. . .
(Fellows)	4,750	7,200	. . .
Fellow E. Tom Herndon William Shields	(3,000) (3,000)	(3,000) (3,000)	3,000 3,000
(Technicians and Technical Assistants)	5,163	5,016	. . .
Research Technician I	(3,150)	(3,000)	2,892
Laboratory Helper Robert Wright	(1,920)	(2,064)	2,172
Senior Secretary Juanita Epperson	3,150	3,480	3,648
Secretary Lee Robertson	2,700	3,024	3,168
Maintenance and Equipment	5,500	5,500	7,500
Total Expenditure Total Budget	$42,437 . . .	. . . $46,591	. . . $51,880

(a) Also $4,400 from Southwestern Medical Foundation; total salary for twelve months, $15,000.
(b) Also $600 from Southwestern Medical Foundation; total salary for twelve months, $6,600 in 1954-55 and $8,000 in 1955-56.

State Budget for Fiscal 1955–1956.

The state budget appropriation was $51,880; the remainder of the $56,880 budget came from Southwestern Medical Foundation—including $4,400 of Dr. Pritchard's salary.

The new Parkland Memorial Hospital was fine as far as bricks and mortar went, but was barely functional because of a lack of personnel and equipment. A brand new building without air conditioning! Oh, there was some air conditioning in the administrative areas but not in the patient areas. I tried to buy a couple of window units for use by the housestaff and their families when they were hospitalized. The senior administrator, Al Scheidt, became very upset, "You are not going to hang those cheese boxes on the outside of my beautiful new hospital!"

**Parkland Memorial Hospital on Harry Hines Boulevard—
circa 1955.**

From Dallas Medical Images, Parkland Memorial Hospital Collection (pmh_ 00003). Creator—Bill Edwards.

Heat could be lethal. Sick patients died from hyperthermia when outside temperatures rose to well above 100°F or more, and mercury thermometer readings were grossly inaccurate. When we finally tried to open the windows to cool things down, we found that many of them would not open. When a story revealing these dangerous shortcomings appeared in the local newspaper,[56] it came as a shock to many who had urged the building of this new city/county hospital.

Another dreadful thing that was not talked about was an apparent agreement that the new hospital would accept all the colored obstetric patients from the community. (Federal legislation finally ended that practice.) For employees, there were separate colored and white entrances. There were also separate colored and white dining rooms and coffee shops, hospital beds, lavatories, drinking fountains, and showers.[57] I had hired two technicians,[58] one colored and one white. They worked together intimately and were close friends on the job. I encouraged them to "integrate" every function they went to and if there were complaints to let me know. I heard of none!

PRENATAL CARE

Old Parkland Hospital was across the street from the shacks, and it was still being used for the Ob/Gyn Clinics. What a mess! Obstetric patients were direct to Old Parkland for prenatal care but not before the fourth month of pregnancy. I was told that by waiting until the fourth month nonpregnant women would be less likely clutter the clinic. Amazingly, there was no workable appointment system. Patients not seen that day were directed to return the next day and start

---

[56] Heat Stroke Kills Man in Hospital. *The Dallas Morning News*. 1956 Aug 8;Part 3, p. 1 (Col 1). Although the man's temperature rose to 106°, autopsy attributed the death to blood clots in the lung according to the evening *Dallas Times Herald*—Lung Clot, Not Heat, Held Cause of Man's Death—1956 Aug 8;B-3 (col 2).

[57] The "separate but equal" doctrine was abolished by federal legislation— Civil Rights Act (1964), Voting Rights Act (1965), and Fair Housing Act (1968)—following the Civil Rights Movement.

[58] The technicians were Gwen Reed Chase and Ruble Ann Mason. Their names appear on the 1957–1958 budget.

over. There were never enough places for all the women to sit. The clinic was in the basement with no air conditioning, high humidity, and temperatures could get to 100°F or even higher. A unique health care team had evolved to care for those pregnant women who became syncopal.[59] Junior medical students rotated as a "faint team" whose function was to diagnose and treat the fainting victims. No wonder prenatal care was not eagerly sought.

There were city and county health department clinics scattered throughout the community which presumably provided prenatal care but didn't. A first-year obstetric resident staffed the outlying clinics. Prenatal care consisted mostly of a nurse and a clerk whose functions were to (1) count the patient! (Federal funding to the city and county health departments were based especially on a head count from the U.S. Children's Bureau.); (2) collect urine and measure its protein content (never first cleansing the vulva); (3) weigh the patient (never checking the scales for accuracy); (4) check the patient's blood pressure; (5) ask the woman how her baby was and, (6) collect a quarter for the iron pills. When these data had all been collected, the patient was typically chastised for gaining too much weight, prescribed a new starvation diet "for the good of the baby," and given the newest and latest "water pills" to make the pregnancy "normal."

I began to find out a lot about the administration of the Obstetric Outpatient Clinics. There were clinics at Parkland administered by Parkland but not by the city or county health departments. There were clinics run by the City of Dallas Health Department without input from Parkland or the Dallas County Health Department. There were clinics in Dallas County outside the city that were not administered by either Parkland or the City of Dallas. All of the above clinics were presumably administered by the Department of Obstetrics and Gynecology at UT Southwestern, but the Chairman of the department (me) had no authority over the actual operation of any of them.

The same was true for Parkland Ob/Gyn in-patient services, emergency services, and labor and delivery services.

---

[59] Syncopal – the patient becomes faint or blacks out.

The senior administrator at Parkland, Jack Price, always started his comeback with, "You people at the medical school always want something." I tried to make changes initially in antepartum care with little success. Some of the clinic nurses boldly stated, "I do not work for you." I tried to meet with the heads of each clinic but ran into all sorts of roadblocks. One M.D. administrator said that another member of his staff handled the OB clinics but he did not know when she might be available. He had sent her to establish a Leprosy Clinic should a suspected carrier who had jumped ship in Galveston turn up in Dallas County.

Establishment of a sensible policy for weight gain was attempted. The nurses were aghast when they learned of my urging women to gain weight during pregnancy. They were reluctant to abandon the rigid weight gain guidelines. So, how did we achieve some semblance of control? The pharmacist supplying the diuretic pills for weight control would dispense them only with a prescription countersigned by me!

Urine collection had become a ritual. A new city clinic had recently opened designed according to the plans of the clinic administrator, Hal Dewlett, a strong-opinioned, non-obstetrician M.D. His pride and joy was a stall for collecting urine privately. The woman was given a paper cup, and as the previous occupant left the waiting room, the woman would enter, close the door, collect some urine, push open a small window and set the urine on a shelf outside the window. The technician would then pick up the cup and fight her way through a long waiting line. It was chaotic but actually unimportant since we did nothing with the results.

As mentioned before, there was no functional appointment system. If a patient was appointed early in the day for a follow-up examination, she knew she would most likely be seen. If appointed later in day, it was likely she would not be seen. Women who were worried about themselves or their babies would come early so they might be seen even though their appointment times were for the afternoon. The need for a workable appointment system was quite obvious but it was a long time coming.

MAGNESIUM SULFATE ARRIVES AT PARKLAND

The treatment of eclampsia when I arrived at Parkland was to control convulsions with intravenous morphine and after a "cooling off" period try to effect delivery by inducing labor or doing cesarean section. However, the treatment had proven so unsatisfactory that Dr. Mengert, my predecessor, published an editorial, which recommended using nothing, claiming that the medications being used only worsened maternal and fetal depression.[60]

At my first Friday noon obstetric housestaff conference, I elected to have a "dry run" on how we were going to manage eclampsia. We no sooner filled our lunch plates when the phone rang. "A woman with eclampsia is in emergency." I said we would all be right there. That morning on the way in, I had dropped off my protocol for managing eclampsia along with some magnesium sulfate solution.

I took over active treatment which emphasized arrest of convulsions with magnesium sulfate, lowering the severely elevated blood pressure with apresoline, and oxygenation of the patient who was undoubtedly acidotic[61] following her series of convulsions. The patient awoke and her confusion lessened.

We turned our attention to the fetus who had tolerated the ordeal fairly well. After a few hours uterine contractions were detected and the cervix was becoming effaced.[46] We used low concentration oxytocin and spontaneously delivered a minimally depressed infant.[36] Intravenous apresoline controlled her severe hypertension, and magnesium sulfate prevented further convulsions. This patient's outcome was the "death knell" for the use of morphine in the treatment of eclampsia at Parkland Hospital.

My predecessor, Dr. Mengert, was especially interested in

---

[60] Maternal/fetal depression – pale appearance and slowing of normal functions, *e.g.*, shallow breathing, slow heart rate, etc.

[61] Acidotic – abnormal increase in the acidity of the body's fluids.

anemia in pregnancy and in cephalopelvic disproportion.[62] He had established regimens, though faulty, for diagnosing and treating both. Hemoglobin concentration was measured on each new obstetric patient. If it was less than 10 gram per 100 milliliters, the woman was scheduled for "prophylactic" transfusion. If there was no break in protocol, *i.e.* if she followed directions, she would show up at the new hospital, enter the transfusion room, lie down, receive 500 milliliters of blood and promptly leave. If she returned to the clinic as directed, the hemoglobin level was rechecked and if still below 10 grams per 100 milliliters, another unit was transfused.

One of several problems was the accuracy of the hemoglobin measurements. The bloods were most often drawn in the morning but not checked until later in the day. Often the blood was not mixed prior to removing the sample from near the top of the tube. With the normal increase in sedimentation rate during pregnancy, a false low hemoglobin level would likely result. Since the samples were measured by visually matching the standard hemoglobin solution against the patient's diluted blood, the likelihood of error on the low side was considerable. (One nurse at one outlying clinic did most of the determinations even though she was legally blind!) Iron was dispensed but its importance was never stressed. Besides, the patients were reluctant to pay 25 cents for 50 tablets of the medication.[63] They needed the money for bus fare to get to Parkland. Lots of work was required to sort out all of these errors and get them corrected. This led to extensive hematologic investigations over the next several years, primarily by Dan Scott, Peggy Whalley, and me.

In the 12 months before I became chairman, we determined that one unit of blood had been transfused for every two pregnancies delivered. Most of it went into the antepartum women who were captured by the 10-gram rule. In 1956, the year after I became chairman, the transfusion rate was 9.34 deliveries per unit of blood transfused! One of our Ob/Gyn residents, Charles Hunt, was a co-author on a

---

[62] Cephalopelvic disproportion – a condition where the mother's pelvis (birth canal) is too small to accommodate the baby's head.

[63] To put this cost in perspective, 25¢ for 50 pills in 1955 would be equivalent to about $2.18 in 2013 (That is an increase from ½ ¢ to ~4⅓ ¢ per pill.)

publication which outlined the lowering of the need for these transfusions, one of the earliest studies performed in Dallas.[64]

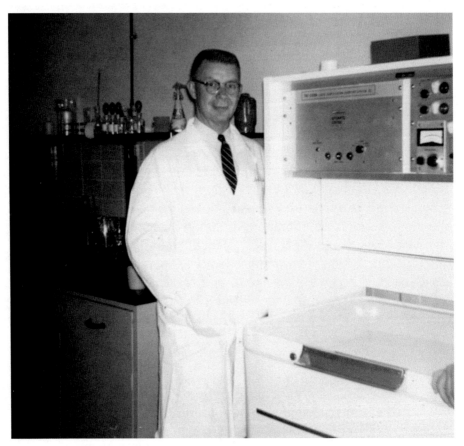

**Professor Jack A. Pritchard, M.D., in his laboratory
at Parkland in 1962**

From Dallas Medical Images, UT Southwestern Collection (uts_00135. Creator—Unknown

I set up a laboratory to screen for hematologic abnormalities on all obstetric patients. The two technicians I had hired shortly after arriving in Dallas, Ruble Mason and Gwen Chase, were superb at de-

---

[64] Pritchard JA, Hunt CF. A comparison of the hematologic responses following the routine prenatal administration of intramuscular and oral iron. *Surg Gynecol Obstet.* 1958 May; 106(5):516-518.

tecting deviations from so-called normal levels. We soon had a group of pregnant women identified to be healthy but hematologically different. Most women cooperated very well with the serial studies that we carried out and served to shed light on the confusing obstetric hematology. Most of the housestaff became interested and actively participated in the studies. Numerous well-received publications followed.

All nulliparous[65] patients were scheduled for x-ray pelvimetry to determine whether there was any cephalopelvic disproportion.[62] Various measurements were done and pelvic capacity was calculated.[66] If it was below a certain "volume", the woman was sent to the Dystocia[67] Clinic where several people looked at the data and examined the pelvis. Typically, if the patient had progressed this far in the scheme, she was scheduled for cesarean section. Many delivered spontaneously before an operating room could be obtained. Obviously, more work was needed in this area.

RECRUITMENT OF FACULTY AND STAFF

We gradually hired some well-trained faculty and staff for the department. It was difficult because of poor stipends and long hours of hard work. At many hospitals, night call meant, "Climb into bed and get up once or twice." At Parkland, it meant you were up and working almost continuously until the next morning when you moved over to your full-time day job.

---

[65] Nulliparous – women who have not been pregnant previously.

[66] The procedure for calculating pelvic capacity—sometimes referred to as *Mengert's measures*—had been published in the *Journal of the American Medical Society* in 1948. See: Mengert WF. Estimation of pelvic capacity. *JAMA* 1948 Sep 18;128(3):169-174.

[67] Dystocia – a difficult labor/delivery in which the baby's head does not descend into the mother's birth canal, either because the cervix has not expanded (dilated) adequately or the mother's pelvis is too small to accommodate the infant's head.

We continued to hunt for talented people. Our first addition was Reuben Adams,[68] a recently graduated senior resident who signed on as an Assistant Professor. In addition to his Ob/Gyn residency training, he had spent time in a medicine residency. He was a solid hand! Later he served as the Chief of Ob/Gyn at Baylor University Hospital in Dallas for many years.

Our reputation as a first-rate training institution was spreading, and we were getting more applicants and acceptances. The first resident selected after my arrival in Dallas was Harwin "Jack" Jamison who wanted to learn all about Ob/Gyn "except the science part." He eventually learned to like the science part and actually participated in some of the ongoing studies. As I associated more with the housestaff, I began to appreciate the enthusiasm of the typical Texan for the practice of Ob/Gyn.

To help provide staffing we set up a training program for medical students so they could function as surgical scrub nurses. This proved effective except for one aspect. The administration did not wish to pay them for this service. We compromised, and a similar program was developed in Anesthesia. The just-finished third-year medical student would spend the summer "learning the trade" and then during his senior year he would serve one night a week as the primary source of OB anesthesia under the direction of the staff anesthesiologist. Many students who at the outset had given no thought to a career in Anesthesia ended up specializing. Our son, David, was one. He finished medical school, spent time on the medical housestaff at Parkland, and then did an anesthesia residency at the University of California at San Francisco.

---

[68] Ruben H. Adams, Jr., began his residency in OB/Gyn at Parkland Memorial Hospital under Dr. William F. Mengert on January 1, 1954. He continued his training under Dr. Pritchard and was Chief Resident from January 1, 1956–December 31, 1956. He joined the obstetrics and gynecology faculty in January 1957 and became an Assistant Professor the following September. He rose to the rank of Professor in 1966. Dr. Adams served as Chairman of Obstetrics and Gynecology at Baylor University Hospital in Dallas from September 1970 until January 1, 1993. While at Baylor, he continued to serve on the part-time clinical faculty at Southwestern covering services at Parkland until August 31, 1993. Dr. Adams died in 2000 in Dallas, Texas.

I wish I could cite all the residents, fellows, and faculty who contributed to the growth of the department, but there are way too many. I will continue to mention some of them as this narrative progresses. Do not feel badly if you feel you have been left out. Were I in my "Black Jack" persona, I might have mentioned you in connection with a blunder best not recalled, but I have tried to avoid bringing up any of these incidents.[69]

RESIDENTS AND MEDICAL STUDENTS

Our medical students received considerable exposure to obstetrics and gynecology, and most of them really liked the specialty. The drawbacks as I already mentioned were the long, irregular hours and the uncertainty of what the next hour might bring. Nonetheless, we recruited a good number of residents and fellows who then made academic obstetrics and gynecology their life-long career. Two early residents deserve special mention.

Paul C. MacDonald, a brilliant student at Southwestern, had to serve two years in the Navy following his internship. A local general practitioner wanted Paul to get some clinical experience in obstetrics and then join him in Family Practice. The practitioner offered him a decent salary to do this for 6 months. I talked with the Chairman of Medicine, Donald Seldin, who said that the proposed trainee had been an outstanding student.[70] We accepted him, and he went to work immediately.

---

[69] Dr. Pritchard would approach case presentations using "blunders" to illustrate how the case was mishandled. "Remember, you can learn from the mistakes of others."

[70] Paul C. MacDonald graduated from Southwestern Medical School in the class of 1955—the last class to receive all its training in obstetrics and gynecology from William F. Mengert, M.D., Professor and Chairman (1943–1955).

Jack A. Pritchard, M.D., teaching students – circa 1960.
Subjects on blackboard are (1) Hydatid mole[71] and (2) Syncytial endo-metrium.[72]

As the months passed, the trainee became more enamored with Ob/Gyn. And, we wanted him to stay in our program. We "bought him back" from the local practitioner, and Paul became a *bona fide* Ob/Gyn resident for the next three years. He then wanted to do a fellowship in Reproductive Endocrinology. Off he went to Columbia University in New York after convincing the Head, Seymour

---

[71] Hydatid mole (also called *hydatidiform mole*) – a pregnancy where a non-viable, fertilized egg attaches to the uterus and produces a mass of grape-like clusters.

[72] Syncytium – a multinucleated cell; a fusion in which individual cells lose their borders and become one large cell with multiple nuclei.

Leiberman, Ph.D., to accept him. He initially went for one year but stayed on for two. Fortunately, a drug company owed me some money for consultation which I passed on to Paul to pay the rent in Fort Lee, New Jersey.

Paul worked closely with a brilliant Ph.D. biochemist while at Columbia, Pen Siiteri, who was especially interested in estrogen metabolism in humans. He liked the idea of working in Dallas with Paul and our department. We had laboratory space but not much money to fund research. I cleared the tentative hiring of Dr. Siiteri with Dean Gill and the Chairman of Biochemistry at Southwestern, Dr. Tidwell. I thought everything was fine. The Biochemistry Chairman backed down stating that some of his faculty made less than the $7,500 that Siiteri was to receive. Fortunately, the Dean backed me. Siiteri's arrived in Dallas with his wife and 4 children and the 5 MacDonalds also returned. Soon Paul and Fin's investigations of estrogen metabolism resulted in several publications which altered the world's thinking and brought them international recognition. I will have more on Dr. MacDonald and his fellow Parkland residents later.

About that same time, it became clear that a promising career path was not limited to male participants. One female Southwestern Medical School student, Peggy Whalley,[73] wished to practice quality Ob/Gyn and had discussed the possibility of doing so with my predecessor, William Mengert. She was bluntly told by Mengert that women did not belong in academic Ob/Gyn.

I met with her and again with help from the Chairman of Medicine, Dr. Seldin, we outlined a training program that included a medicine internship, a residency in Ob/Gyn and a combined fellowship in Medicine and Ob/Gyn. Her training would be supervised by the Chairmen of both Medicine and Ob/Gyn. This training program called for the full cooperation of the Medicine department and for which Dr. Whalley and I remain grateful. Upon completion she was soon turning down offers of Chairs at other medical schools, but she was needed at Parkland and Southwestern and she stayed. In a short time Peggy

---

[73] Peggy Whalley graduated from Southwestern Medical School in the class of 1956.

Whalley became recognized nationally and internationally for her contributions to the clinical science of Obstetrics and Gynecology and Internal Medicine.

Peggy was convinced that a very sedentary lifestyle promoted fetal well-being in pregnancies where the mother's health was compromised, such as with pregnancy-induced hypertension. An outgrowth of her efforts in this regard became what is referred to as "Peggy's Palace", a ward in Parkland Hospital devoted specifically to caring for women with high-risk pregnancies. Dr. Whalley also collaborated with me on several hematologic studies.[74] I recently spoke with Peggy (2001). She emphasized that although the work was very hard, she enjoyed her obstetrics service. "I really enjoyed being on the faculty!"[75]

Wilford Hall USAF Medical Center in San Antonio was in the process of upgrading to a major teaching hospital shortly after I came to Dallas. I visited there frequently and tried to help with the organization of their training program. I was named National Consultant to the Air Force in 1968 and served in that capacity until 1990 when I assumed emeritus status. We were fortunate to have this affiliation with Wilford Hall. Their residency program always contained an abundance of excellent physicians, many of whom desired fellowship training in maternal-fetal medicine after completing their Ob/Gyn residencies. Most often we were their first choice, and we obtained excellent trainees who then went on to productive careers as departmental chairmen or chiefs of service in medical schools throughout the United States. I was pleased to have worked with John Hauth, Gary

---

[74] Pritchard JA, Whalley PJ. Severe hypokalemia due to prolonged administration of chlorothiazide during pregnancy. Am J Obstet Gynecol. 1961 Jun;81:1241-1244.

Whalley PJ, Pritchard JA, Richards JR Jr. Sickle cell trait and pregnancy. JAMA 1963 Dec 28;186:1132-1135.

[75] Upon her retirement in 1992, Peggy Whalley became the second Professor Emeritus in Obstetrics and Gynecology at UT Southwestern. Dr. Pritchard was the first (1990) and the only one to hold the title Ashbel Smith Professor Emeritus. (See Editor's Addendum page 95.)

Hankins, Larry Gilstrap and Alvin "Bud" Brekken to name a few.[76]

I have watched Bud's clinical and administrative skills since we were both at Parkland many years ago. Together we published an extensive report on placental abruption that is still quoted today.[77] And congratulations to John Hauth who retired from the Air Force, and was recently honored by them with the establishment of the Hauth Perinatal Center at Wilford Hall Hospital in San Antonio.

Other members of our faculty were recruited from unusual backgrounds. For example, Uel Crosby came to us from the Indian Health Service. We literally hired him off the desert in Arizona. He then left to rejoin the Indian Health Service for several more years. Eventually the call of Parkland and Southwestern prevailed, and he returned to Dallas.[78] I will always recall Uel's response to the Assistant Secretary of Health, Education and Welfare who would interrogate him about the Indians. "Tell me this about the Indians, tell me that about the Indians, etc., etc." Uel calmly replied, "Sir, just think of them as people."[79]

---

[76] Following retirement from the Air Force, Drs. Gilstrap and Brekken joined the OB/Gyn faculty at UT Southwestern. Larry Gilstrap went on to become Chairman of Obstetrics and Gynecology at the University of Texas Health Science Center at Houston and in 2010 became the Executive Director of the American Board of Obstetrics and Gynecology (ABOG). Alvin "Bud" Brekken remained in the department until his retirement in June 2001, when he went to work part time for ABOG.

[77] Pritchard JA, Brekken AL. Clinical and laboratory studies on cases of severe abruptios placentae. *Am J Obstet Gynecol.* 1967 Mar 1;97(5):681-700. Placental abruption is defined in footnote 30.

[78] Dr. Crosby served as Associate Director of Maternal Health and Family Planning at UT Southwestern from 1972–1975. He returned to UT Southwestern in 1985 and continued covering Parkland Hospital services until his retirement in August 2010 at age 74.

[79] It is not surprising that Dr. Pritchard liked this story. He felt strongly in the dignity of each individual and in acknowledging the patient as a person with a name—not as a disease. Barry Schwarz, M.D. (class of 1968) recalls Dr. Pritchard's delivering this message to his medical school class one Saturday morning. It was the first time anyone had said anything like that to his class.

   Susan Cox, upon completion of her fellowship in maternal-fetal medicine followed a similar path leaving Southwestern and returning a few years later. She is now a full professor and Assistant Dean for Professional Education.[80]   Karen Bradshaw[81] is another prominent member of the faculty in the subspecialty of reproductive endocrinology. I include these women now to recognize their long-standing academic status.

UT Southwestern Campus viewed from the front—circa 1960

From left to right—Parkland Memorial Hospital, Hoblitzelle Clinical Science Building (back side), and Cary Basic Science Building (foreground in front of Hoblizelle Building.)

From Dallas Medical Images, UT Southwestern Collection (uts_00117). Creator— Unknown.

---

[80] Dr. Cox was named Regional Dean–Austin Programs on July 1, 2011. After completing her fellowship at UT Southwestern in 1988, she joined the faculty. She left in 1990 but returned to UT Southwestern in 1993.

[81] Karen Bradshaw graduated from Southwestern Medical School in 1981 and did a residency in obstetrics and gynecology at Parkland. After completing her reproductive endocrinology fellowship, she left UT Southwestern for a year but returned as an Assistant Professor in 1988. Today (2013), she is Professor and Medical Director for the Lowe Center for Women's Preventative Health Care at UT Southwestern.

New Clinical Science Building—circa 1963

Begun in 1956, construction was completed in 1958. In August, the Department of Obstetrics and Gynecology moved from the shacks to the 5th floor—which it shared with Biomedical Illustration.[82] Dedicated on April 16, 1959, the building was renamed the Karl Hoblitzelle Clinical Science Building on October 7, 1960. The building in the background on the left is the Cary Basic Science Building—the first building (1955) on the new medical school campus.

From Dallas Medical Images, UT Southwestern Collection (uts_ 00124). Creator—Unknown.

   I met Kenneth Leveno while attending a conference at a predominantly private hospital in Phoenix, Arizona. He was the senior resident and was presenting the case of a maternal death transferred from an Indian reservation. Two things impressed me: (1) He was well prepared and (2) he was very upset with the outcome and tried to

---

[82] Juanita Epperson Lambeth letter dated July 9, 2011.

take the blame, which was unjustified. We talked following the conference. He wanted to do a fellowship at a first-rate department but realized that his training to date did not really qualify him.

I invited him to come to Dallas. He did and was interviewed by several staff including Peggy Whalley, director of the maternal-fetal medicine fellowship program. Everyone wished he had a better academic background, but they saw and heard something that favorably impressed them and he was accepted. Dr. Leveno's contributions to clinical investigation over the last three decades have been outstanding. [83]

We also carefully selected five fellows from abroad to train with us: two from Guatemala, two from Germany, and one from Iran. [84] They did not have a lasting desire to become teachers and researchers but did become competent practitioners in Ob/Gyn.

---

[83] Kenneth Leveno did his residency at St. Joseph's Hospital in Phoenix, Arizona. Following his fellowship at Southwestern (1976–1978), he joined the faculty, becoming Professor in 1988, and serving as Chief of the Division of Maternal–Fetal Medicine from 1996–2012. Active in clinical research throughout his career, in 1996, he became the principle investigator for the National Institutes of Health (NIH) Maternal–Fetal Medicine Units Network (MFMU) grant at UT Southwestern. The MFMU, a consortium of university-based medical centers, was created in 1986 to focus on clinical questions related to maternal-fetal medicine and obstetrics—particularly those associated with preterm birth.

[84] The fellows were Juan Jimenez and Rigoberto Santos-Ramos from Guatemala, Johann Duenhoelter and Adolf Schindler from Germany, and Ali Toofanian from Iran. Dr. Toofanian's father had been minister of defense under the Shah.

TRANSFER OF THE *WILLIAMS TEXTBOOK OF OBSTETRICS* TO ITS NEW HOME

I had been invited to attend a meeting of the then prestigious American Gynecologic Society as a guest. The policy for the meeting was a relaxed format between members, candidates for membership, and guests. If all went well both scientifically and socially, the candidate was formally invited to present a paper at a future annual meeting. Formal discussants were appointed and the full society membership voted to accept or not accept the candidate, taking into account their impressions of the guest's presentation and the comments of the discussants. The strain on some of the candidates was unbearable.

Pritchard Family Photo
Dr. Pritchard in his office on the UT Southwestern campus.
Circa—late 1960s

I was formally invited to present to the society and informally advised to leave my wife at home so I could direct all my energies to my presentation and subsequent discussions and personal contacts that might follow. I notified meeting registration that my wife would accompany me to the meeting.

The night before the meeting as we signed into our prestigious hotel, The Homestead, there was a note from Nicholson Eastman, Chairman of Obstetrics at Johns Hopkins Medical School and the Author-Editor of *Williams Textbook of Obstetrics*. He wanted to speak with me in the morning if at all possible. I called him, and we arranged to have breakfast together. He said to bring my wife because "she will have an interest in what I am about to propose." I was sure that I would recognize him although I had only seen him briefly prior to this occasion. I spent a restless night. What did he want?

Even though I was the first speaker that morning, we sat down and he started discussing my career to date and why he wanted to speak with us. He was about to retire, and he wanted to transfer *The Book* to someone "worthy." He had chosen me to inherit the *Williams Textbook of Obstetrics!* It suddenly dawned on me that I was the first speaker that morning! As I started to leave, pointing to my name as first speaker, he said, "Go ahead. I want to talk to your wife alone anyhow."

My presentation that day was about the hematologic changes induced by hydatidiform moles.[71] Most all of the changes in normal pregnancies were also identified with classic hydatidiform moles. The study showed clearly that a fetus was not essential for these changes to occur. What triggers these sizeable hematologic alterations? I do not know.

Meanwhile back to Dr. Eastman. My wife told him that from what she knew she favored the textbook (commonly known as "The Bible") coming to Dallas, but I don't think that she appreciated the workload that this would entail. The pros and cons were discussed.

Even though I was still young, I had been chairman for a long time, and the administrative duties had ground away at my time. Currently at Southwestern there was an extremely capable young man who deserved a chair. If we did not make him chair here, one of the other medical schools that had been courting him would hire him away. If Paul MacDonald were made Chairman, I would be most happy to work only as a Professor of Ob/Gyn and Chief of Obstetrics at Parkland where the delivery load was now approaching 10,000 per year.

The prevailing philosophy in most medical schools at that time was for the new chairman to be selected from another institution rather than from within, to avoid in-breeding.

However, the new President of Southwestern, Charles Sprague, approved this "rotation" of the chair. With that settled, I was able to take on the duties as author/editor of *Williams Textbook of Obstetrics*.[85]

The President was happy with this arrangement. I even received a sizeable raise as well as being named Ashbel Smith Professor of Ob/Gyn.[86] (Ashbel Smith was Sam Houston's Surgeon General.) I also promised to continue to head the community-wide family planning project that I had initiated until it was firmly established under the Goals for Dallas Program.

---

[85] Dr. Pritchard was listed as a collaborator on the 13th edition (1966) edited by Nicholson J. Eastman and Louis M. Hellman. He co-authored the 14th edition (1971) with Louis M. Hellman from Johns Hopkins and actually did most of the work according to department sources. He was the senior author/editor for the 15th–17th editions with Paul C. MacDonald as his co-author. Norman F. Gant was added as a co-author on the 17th edition. Beginning with the 18th edition, F. Gary Cunningham became the senior author/editor— a position he still holds today (2013).

[86] This honor came in 1985. See Editor's Addendum on page 95.

OB/Gyn Archives — J Wagers Photo

Williams Obstetrics—The Pritchard Editions[85]

CHAIRMAN PAUL C. MACDONALD, M.D.

My protégé, Paul MacDonald, not only accepted the Chair of Ob/Gyn but agreed to co-author *Williams Textbook of Obstetrics*, a most worthy addition.[87] Paul was as outstanding an individual as I had ever met in academic Ob/Gyn. The department continued to flourish under his leadership. He received a prestigious career development award from the National Institute of Child Health and Human Development. Through the years, he continued to exhibit the vigorous leadership that I once did until he, too, was nearly consumed by the intense effort required to maintain a first-rate academic department. He was now spending an inordinate amount of time in administration. We all coaxed him to become Director of the newly established Cecil H. and Ida Green Center for Reproductive Biology Sciences. He stepped down as Chairman and ran the Green Center with skills possessed by only a few. He remained its Director until his death in November 1997.[88]

A minor point, but flattering nonetheless, was the approach once used by Johns Hopkins Medical School in searching for a new chairman. The chairman of their search committee met with both Paul and me in Dallas. He stated bluntly, "I am here to hire one of you as our new Chairman and to stay in Dallas until I do. One of you please say 'yes'!" He finally gave up and left. Both of us stayed in Dallas, and the *Williams Textbook of Obstetrics* did not return to Baltimore.

---

[87] During 1969–1970, Paul MacDonald served as Acting Chairman while Dr. Pritchard worked on *Williams Obstetrics*. Dr. MacDonald was Chairman of Obstetrics and Gynecology from September 1970 through December 1976. In 1970, he became Director of the newly created Center for Reproductive Biology Sciences at UT Southwestern. In February 1974, the Center was renamed the Cecil H. and Ida Green Center for Reproductive Biology Sciences following the Green's endowment of a distinguished chair for Dr. MacDonald, the Center's Director.

[88] Paul MacDonald died of disseminated carcinoma at his home in Dallas, Texas on November 24, 1997 at age 67.

ESTABLISHMENT OF A COMMMUNITY-WIDE FAMILY PLANNING
PROGRAM

A novel program, Goals for Dallas, was being formulated
through the efforts of many of the distinguished citizens of the community and headed by Mayor Erik Jonsson, one of the founders of
Texas Instruments. The Goals for Dallas Program consisted of all the
community improvements that Dallas needed to make to become a
"City of Excellence." What goals needed to be achieved to make Dallas a truly great city? One was to provide comprehensive health care
for the indigent and near-indigent residents of Greater Dallas. Of particular importance was the establishment of an effective family planning program to be administered by Southwestern Medical School
and supported by a combination of local, regional, and national funding as well as sizeable private philanthropy. The President of Southwestern Medical School, Charles Sprague, accepted this challenge
and agreed to involve the medical school in the establishment and
day-to-day operation of this worthwhile endeavor. It is almost certainly the school's involvement in this important mission that led to
endowments from the citizens who could now witness the benefits of
such a town-gown relationship.

I was appointed to head the Greater Dallas Family Planning
Program with full support from the President's Office as well as that of
the Chairman of the Goals for Dallas Program.[89] The appropriation of
sizeable funds from Congress to establish effective family planning
program was a blessing. It did require the participation of a number of
organizations that individually were reluctant to commit but we involved them successfully by including their budgets as part of the
matching funds that would be used to support the family planning clinics. In 1969, we received a pleasant surprise. Not only were we
awarded the amount requested but soon after a supplemental grant to

---

[89] Erik Jonsson served as Chairman of Goals for Dallas from 1965 until 1976
when he became Chairman Emeritus.

http://www.ti.com/corp/docs/company/history/timeline/key/1990/images/6501
2-1.pdf

further expand our facilities! The Office of the Chairman of the Goals for Dallas followed our progress closely. It became obvious that this project was considered a major goal of this program!

My wife and I set out to locate clinic sites throughout the city in areas that desperately needed them. Parkland Hospital administration had pledged Ob/Gyn personnel and facilities as matching funds for the clinic operations as had the city and county health departments. We needed more clinics and quickly!

Our first search uncovered a site in a fairly new but struggling shopping mall in South Dallas. An empty Singer Sewing Machine sales room and mini-warehouse proved satisfactory as our first location. Signe and I, armed with measuring tapes and several rolls of masking tape, laid out a floor plan that we felt would suit our needs. The medical school Business Office agreed to pay for all the expenditures out of the federal grant as long as they were designated specifically for the family planning clinics.

At one of the city health department clinic sites, we installed a large house trailer,[90] paid for from our grant which provided much needed additional space. It was a bargain. Another clinic site considered part of the city health department consisted of a large, quaintly attractive cobblestone building that had in the past served primarily as a Venereal Disease Clinic but was now mostly used for storage of "junk." The interior had been converted into a series of cubicles just big enough for a small desk and two chairs. We discovered that if we knocked out alternate partitions, the enlarged rooms could accommodate examining tables for women.

The ownership of the building, however, was in doubt. The WPA[91] had built it during the Depression and it was on city property. It had been pledged as part of matching funds for the Family Planning

---

[90] The trailer was at the Oak Cliff Lions Club clinic according to Barry E. Schwarz, M.D., who saw patients there. (Conversation: 9 August 2012).

[91] WPA was the Works Project Administration. Part of President Franklin Delano Roosevelt's New Deal, it employed millions of unskilled people in public works projects throughout the United States between 1935 and 1943.

Program. I brought in an axe and a few other tools from home and started to remove the alternate partitions. Soon, the phone rang and someone in city government was threatening me with arrest. I tried to explain that we had 45 women appointed to be seen in this clinic in two days. I urged him to come out to the building and we would go over the problem together. He said he would send his assistant. As far as I know, no such individual ever visited the site. A janitor who appeared from nowhere played a major role in helping clear up the mess and cleaned up the space very nicely thereafter.

Pritchard Family Photo

Original Southeast Dallas Women's Clinic in Wahoo Park.
Sometimes called the Wahoo Clinic, the floor had dry rot and bulged in the middle so people were constantly walking up hill or down hill.[92]

We discovered that the costs of tubal sterilization would be covered by our grant. With no one at the hospital business office now pressuring women for full payment, this procedure became very popular. We learned that vasectomies could be paid for, too. However,

---

[92] From Barry E. Schwarz, M.D., in 25 June 2012 email.

when I approached the head of the Urology department,[93] he did not wish to participate. His residents learned of this, and pressured him into participation, for a fee from the grant, of course. Relatively soon we had a complete Family Planning Service with eight clinics located throughout Dallas County and available to all who wanted to be seen, even on Saturday. In the year 2000, 52,254 patient visits were made to the eight Family Planning Clinics.[94]

We developed a very simple but effective technique for tubal sterilization in which a midsegment of oviduct was resected and the cut ends were ligated and left free-standing rather than the 2 stumps being tied together with the risk of anastomosis[95] and recanalization.[96] The failure rate for this new technique was very low (less than 1 in 400). Around the country this technique has become known as the Parkland procedure. It replaced the old Madlener technique that had a failure rate of 7%. No wonder women complained that tubals did not work.

A higher failure rate was reported by Johns Hopkins when sterilization was done at the time of cesarean section rather than postpartum. This made no sense! We repeated their study and found no evidence of a higher failure rate with cesarean section.[97] We effectively stopped this rumor through the collection and review of charts by Signe and a resident, Milton Husbands. We often solicited help from medical students, residents, and even faculty wives in our research efforts.

We continued to open more clinics to meet the demands for family planning services until we had a total of eight plus Parkland. Race and religion did not deter our patients from using the clinics

---

[93] Harry M. Spence was head of Urology from 1946 until 1971.

[94] In 2011, there were 73,528 patient visits to Parkland's Family Planning Clinics.

[95] Anastomosis – reconnection.

[96] Recanalization – restoration of the flow in a previously interrupted channel.

[97] Husbands ME Jr., Pritchard JA, Pritchard SA. Failure of tubal sterilization accompanying cesarean section. *Am J Obstet Gynecol.* 1970 Jul 15;107(6): 966-967.

even though we were told to anticipate physical violence by Black males who especially opposed the concept of family planning for Black women. Our only casualty was a window at one of the clinics broken by a boy swinging a bottle tied to the end of a rope that broke while he was swinging it briskly through the air. Dallas remained free of the riots that plagued other large cities.

At the time the Greater Dallas Family Planning Clinic Program opened, an increasing variety of agents and intrauterine devices appeared on the scene. Their safety, however, had not always been thoroughly investigated. Our clinics eventually supplied data that allowed us to either proceed with the use of the agent or to promptly remove it if adverse effects were identified.

The dedication of the Ob/Gyn staff to good health care was borne out by our experiences with an intrauterine device known as the Majzlin Spring. Although it had been used in at least one other large clinic in Brooklyn, NY with excellent results according to a publication, it proved to be a disaster in our patients. The heavy metallic spring would cut into the cervix and body of the uterus leading to pain, pelvic infection, and anemia. Often the spring could not be removed manually even with anesthesia. We did succeed in removing all of the 410 springs – some surgically – that we had inserted. One patient was traced to central Mexico where one of our staff removed the spring and replaced it with the copper T model. (We had very few problems with the copper T.)

I remain confused by the disparate results obtained on this device from Dallas and Brooklyn. The experience in Dallas was horrendous. The device worked its way into the body of the uterus causing gross bleeding and pelvic cellulitis.[98] I do not know if the Chairman at Brooklyn ever knew about this dichotomy of results. A short time after our report appeared in *Obstetrics and Gynecology*,[99] he visited Dallas and happened to be sitting in my office when I received a phone call from the Federal District Attorney of New York. The attorney wanted

---

[98] Cellulitis – a localized or diffuse inflammation of tissue.

[99] Taylor WW, Martin FG, Pritchard SA, Pritchard JA. Complications from Majzlin spring intrauterine device. *Obstet Gynecol.* 1973 Mar;41 (3):404-413.

to alert me that on the basis of our publication his office was seizing all Majzlin springs including those at the site of manufacture. He said I should anticipate calls from the wire services and might want to be prepared. I hung up and the visiting chairman from Brooklyn asked whom I had been speaking to. I became vague and told him I would call the party back as it involved a malpractice suit. We never heard anything more. The Chairman at Brooklyn became the Deputy Assistant Secretary of Health, Education and Welfare in charge of family planning. Perhaps this provided a shield.

In the beginning, our patients had heard that birth control pills were dangerous. After several months of dispensing them, however, word spread that they were "great." Concern was expressed by "authorities" that women who developed hypertension during pregnancy were at increased risk of becoming hypertensive while taking oral contraceptives. We evaluated a large number of women who became hypertensive during pregnancy and then normotensive after delivery and who were given the pill for contraception. Recurrent hypertension was rare. Included in the study were 26 eclamptic women, none of whom became hypertensive when started on the pill.[100] We could, therefore, assure our family planning patients that they were not at serious risk of high blood pressure if they took the pill.

I decided early on that nurses with Ob/Gyn experience would play an important role in providing family planning services. I thought that we could train people sufficiently to allow them to even insert intrauterine devices. Our senior nurses were most receptive to this proposal once we made it clear that they would be trained before help was recruited outside the system. For example, I would take a senior nurse supervisor with me to one of the more remote clinic sites for "inspection" but as long as we were there we would each insert a device. Once the senior nurse felt confident, she typically readily accepted that her role in these clinics would be more than just filling out forms and dispensing birth control pills.

---

[100] Pritchard JA, Pritchard SA. Blood pressure response to estrogen-progestin oral contraceptives after pregnancy-induced hypertension. *Am J Obstet Gynecol.* 1977 Dec 1;129(7):733-739.

The Greater Dallas Family Planning Program was an immediate success and this success has persisted through the years.[101] In 2000, there were 52,000 plus patient visits to these clinics.

PRESIDENT KENNEDY

One uneventful night in 1963, I spoke to a group of obstetricians in Kansas City and returned to Dallas the next morning. The pilot told us we were going to go straight in to Love Field and deplane quickly in order to clear the runway for Air Force One because President Kennedy was visiting Dallas that day. There were lots of police, and we were rushed out of the terminal.

I had a luncheon conference scheduled with our junior students followed by a cesarean hysterectomy. I went to my office to check in and returned to the hospital through Emergency Services. There was much confusion. The President's car was there, and he had just been taken inside. A medical student was crying, "The President is dead. His brains were running out!"[102] I went up the back stairs to the operating room where our surgery was scheduled.

---

[101] The Family Planning Program had a series of medical directors who contributed to its success. Initially, there was Dr. Johanna Perlmutter, followed by Uel Crosby, Walter Taylor, Michael Sims, and Barry Schwarz. (Dr. Schwarz trained with Dr. Perlmutter.) In 1974, Stephen Heartwell, D.Ph., was hired to administer the program. Dr. Heartwell had been affiliated with the family planning program in Louisiana and had experience in obtaining funding. According to Dr. Schwarz, the program "took off" under Dr. Heartwell's leadership. But it was really the partnership between Heartwell, the administrator, and Schwarz, the medical director, that created the successful operation. The two teamed to find cost-effective ways to deliver family planning services without compromising medical care. And they succeeded. In 2006, Parkland Health and Hospital System took over the operation of the Family Planning Clinics. Dr. Schwarz remained with the program as the Chief of Service for Family Planning at Parkland—a position he holds today (2013).

[102] John F. Kennedy was killed on November 22, 1963.

Governor, John Connolly, needed surgery badly. As our case was elective, it was postponed, and the surgeons took over the facilities to operate on the Governor. He was exsanguinating[103] from several severed blood vessels. Once blood was transfused vigorously and the bleeding arrested, the Governor rallied. He later told me that he was sure he was dying. He was most impressed by the overall operation of the medical school and Parkland Hospital. He was convinced that the medical school was underfunded and this deficit should be corrected. He made sure that it was.

During the course of my rounds, I went to the labor and delivery area and found things to be under control and all posts were appropriately staffed. As I was leaving to return to surgery, I met a reporter who was desperately looking for a telephone to call Washington and inform his office of the President's assassination. I led him to a pay phone near my lab which had not yet been discovered. Fortunately, I had coins for him to make the call since he did not. I believe he was Merriman Smith of the White House Press Corps.[104]

I tried again to return to the operating suite. As I started through the large swinging doors, I was pushed against the wall and a voice barked, "Let the First Lady through." I was held there until the nursing supervisor who was standing guard identified me.

Many people and groups reviewed the quality of care available that day at Parkland Memorial Hospital. The only shortcoming they could find was that the walls in the Emergency Unit could have used some paint. Interestingly, painting had just been authorized at the Medical Advisory Council meeting just a few nights before.

---

[103] Exsanguinating – bleeding, which if uncheck will result in death.

[104] A. Merriman Smith (1913–1970) was the White House reporter for United Press International (UPI) who broke the story of shots being fired at President Kennedy in Dealey Plaza. He beat Jack Bell of the Associated Press (AP) to the radio-telephone in the wire service car.
http://www.arlingtoncemetery.net/albertme.htm

PRESBYTERIAN HOSPITAL

A new private hospital, Presbyterian,[105] was being promoted especially by residents of North Dallas, an area rapidly filling with young families of childbearing age. This created quite a stir since the lay sponsors hoped the University of Texas Southwestern Medical School would supply personnel and funding to help finance the operation. The chairman of each of the medical school departments would be responsible for selecting a chief of his service who would, in turn, be in charge of the day-to-day operations at Presbyterian.

In Ob/Gyn, this created ill-will among several practitioners who were interested in hospital privileges. I nominated a senior Ob/Gyn practitioner, William Devereaux, who was respected in the medical and lay communities. In his capacity as temporary chief, however, he was never able to coax a significant number of pregnant women and their doctors to come to Presbyterian to make the funding plan viable.

Important lay members of the hospital board, all of whom had donated money for construction and operation of the new hospital, as well as the hospital administrator, wanted someone else as Chief of Ob/Gyn – Dr. William Guerrero. In speaking with several of those opposed to his appointment, they indicated that they would not actively support the hospital if he were named Chief of Ob/Gyn. We were locked in a windowless room in the Republic National Bank building in which – according to the chairman of the hospital board – we would stay until the matter was resolved. Most all of the other town-gown conflicts I had inherited had been resolved to the satisfaction of the majority of the Ob/Gyn practitioners. Appointing Dr. William Guerrero as Chief of Ob/Gyn at the struggling, new Presbyterian Hospital looked as if it might re-ignite these old grievances.

---

[105] The 300-bed Presbyterian Hospital of Dallas opened in May 1966 on the site that had been the Reynolds Presbyterian Orphanage since 1923. After seven years of planning, in 1962, a successful fund drive raised $4,678,440 from more than 5,000 donors to build the hospital.
http://www.texashealth.org/body.cfm?id=2108

But, wait a minute! The medical school had appointed me Chairman of the Ob/Gyn, as young as I was, and it had proven a good choice insofar as the town-gown relationship was concerned. Why not make a comparable appointment age-wise to fill the position of Chief of Ob/Gyn at Presbyterian? Dr. William Guerrero had a nephew, Charles, who was well-trained in clinical obstetrics and gynecology, was well-liked by his fellow Ob/Gyn practitioners, and was already practicing at Presbyterian. So, when the lay chairman of the hospital board demanded a name, I replied, "Dr. Guerrero – that is, Dr. Charles Guerrero, the nephew of Dr. William Guerrero." No one was prepared for this selection. I suspect that the senior Dr. Guerrero was prepared to shoot down any nominee, but how could he contest the nomination of his own nephew? No one openly challenged Charles Guerrero's nomination and a crisis was avoided. The Ob/Gyn service at Presbyterian thrived. Eventually Dr. Dan Scott,[106] Professor of Ob/Gyn at Southwestern, became the full-time Chief and Dr. Charles Guerrero continued on in private practice at Presbyterian.

F. GARY CUNNINGHAM JOINS THE DEPARTMENT

Abe Mickal, for many years the Chairman of Ob/Gyn at Louisiana State University Medical School in New Orleans, was planning to retire in the near future and expressed his desires regarding his successor. Abe had been an All-American quarterback and even a member of the state legislature in his student days. He contacted me about the possibility of a recent graduate of their residency program, F. Gary Cunningham, spending a year working with us at Southwestern. Gary participated in everything, and we had a very rewarding year. Toward the end of his time with us, Gary asked if he could stay in Dallas and complete the equivalent of a Maternal-Fetal Medicine fellowship and perhaps, join our faculty. We were pleased to grant

---

[106] Daniel E. Scott, a 1961 graduate of Southwestern Medical School, did an OB/Gyn residency at Parkland (1962–1964), followed by a one-year fellowship. He joined the faculty in 1970 and was Chief of Service at Presbyterian Hospital from 1974 until his retirement the end of December 1997.

him this request, but emphasized that he – not us – would have to inform Dr. Mickal of his change of plans.

Gary stayed and eventually became chairman of the department in 1982, when Norman Gant who had followed Paul MacDonald as chairman, asked to be relieved of his position. Since then Norman has directed his energies and management skills towards the full-time operation of the American Board of Obstetrics and Gynecology. He is now Executive Director of this organization and is doing an excellent job. Congratulations, Norman![107]

I had the opportunity to work with Gary until my retirement from the department [108] and have continued to follow his career. He has served as Chief of Obstetrics at Parkland and Chairman of the department, all the while serving as senior author/editor and keeping a firm, guiding hand on *Williams Textbook of Obstetrics,* now in its 21st edition.

Gary actively teaches, does meaningful research, recruits residents, staff and faculty and tolerates administration. All of these efforts, along with those of his colleagues have helped to maintain the Department of Ob/Gyn at the University of Texas Southwestern Medical Center as one of the best in the country. Gary continues to demonstrate a vitality that should keep him in office for a long time to come. Let's not tamper with success![109]

---

[107] Norman F. Gant, M.D., was Chairman of Obstetrics and Gynecology from 1977 through May 1983. He was Executive Director of the American Board of Obstetrics and Gynecology from 1992 until his retirement December 31, 2009. Following his retirement, he was appointed Professor Emeritus of Obstetrics and Gynecology (January 2010).

[108] Dr. Pritchard retired August 31, 1990, and became Ashbel Smith Professor Emeritus of Obstetrics and Gynecology.

[109] F. Gary Cunningham, M.D., was Chairman of Obstetrics and Gynecology from 1982 through 2004—first as interim and then as chair effective September 1983. He remained on the faculty after stepping down as chair and continued to cover the high-risk obstetrical service at Parkland. Beginning with the 18th edition, he assumed the reins as senior author/editor of *Williams Obstetrics* and fittingly dedicated the 18th edition to Dr. Pritchard. (The 23rd edition of *Williams Obstetrics* was published in 2010, and the 24th edition will be

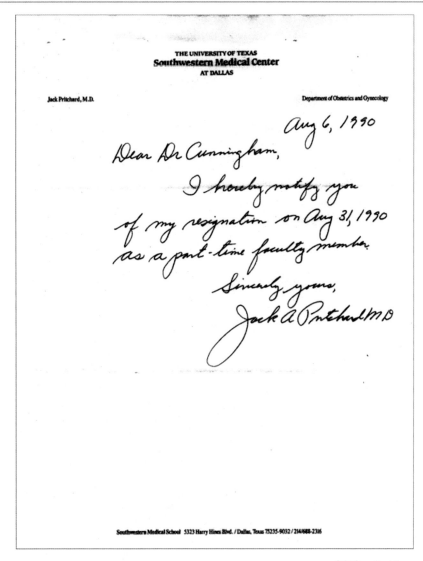

THE UNIVERSITY OF TEXAS
Southwestern Medical Center
AT DALLAS

Jack Pritchard, M.D.

Department of Obstetrics and Gynecology

Aug 6, 1990

Dear Dr Cunningham,

I hereby notify you of my resignation on Aug 31, 1990 as a part-time faculty member.

Sincerely yours,

Jack A Pritchard MD

Southwestern Medical School 5323 Harry Hines Blvd. / Dallas, Texas 75235-9032 / 214/688-2316

OB/Gyn Archives

Dr. Pritchard's letter of resignation.

Handwritten and to the point, this letter is an excellent example of Dr. Pritchard's straightforward approach. Not one to renege on an obligation, his resignation was effective at the end of his annual contract.

published in 2014.) Under his leadership in 2008, Dr. Cunningham's vision for a companion textbook for gynecologists was realized with the publication of *Williams Gynecology*. (The 2nd edition was published in 2012).

QUINTUPLETS

The birth of the Davis quintuplets at Parkland Hospital 26 years ago [July 18, 1975][110] and their subsequent normal development gave the hospital and the medical school an abundance of favorable publicity then and at their annual birthday parties. No quintuplets had been born in Texas and at the time of their birth, the survival of all quintuplets was very uncommon.

Reunion with a famous five.

Picture of the first quintuplets born in Texas at reception held in their honor at Southwestern Medical School shortly after their first birthday. Dr. Jack Pritchard (left), Professor of Obstetrics and Gynecology; Debbie Davis (center), babies' mother; and Dr. Charles Rosenfeld (right), Assistant Professor of Pediatrics and Obstetrics and Gynecology. Photo from *Newsletter*, University of Texas Health Science Center at Dallas – September 1976. © UT Southwestern Medical Center.

---

[110] This manuscript was written in 2001. In 2013, the Quints celebrated their 38th birthdays. Two other sets of quintuplets have been delivered by faculty physicians who received their fellowship training at UT Southwestern. On June 19, 1998, four boys and a girl were born to Victor and Sonia Zuniga at Parkland Memorial Hospital; delivered by a team led by Ronald Ramus. On August 9, 2012, Patricia Santiago-Muñoz led a team at St. Paul University Hospital that delivered three boys and two girls to Gavin and Carrie Jones.

Our major concerns were maternal health which should improve following their birth as well as fetal dysmaturity[111] and prematurity. Mrs. Davis had developed severe preeclampsia.[13,4] We knew there were four fetuses from the ultrasound examination, and we knew the gestational age of the fetuses since the time of fertilization was known quite precisely. At 31.5 weeks, we decided that the risks to the fetuses from further unhealthy intrauterine existence exceeded the risks from prematurity. This is a challenge that obstetricians and neonatologists often face but rarely in such an overwhelming dose. We, however, were dealing with the welfare of four infants (that we knew of) who, if they all survived the challenge of prematurity, would have a total lifespan of 300 years.

On July 18, 1975, we performed a cesarean section and delivered not 4 but 5 infants – four girls and a boy. Even though their gestational age was identical, their sizes varied from as small as 1 pound 14 ounces (860 grams) to as large as 3 pounds 10 ounces (1530 grams). The smallest and most dysmature infant was not suspected and was found as the large placenta was being extracted. A fifth resuscitation team was quickly assembled but was hardly needed. Transient respiratory distress developed only in the largest infant, a boy. All of the quintuplets thrived. We have kept in touch with all 5 over the last 26 years and have been most pleased by their normal development. The mother soon shed the vestiges of preeclampsia and was once again an attractive 19-year-old woman who subsequently went on to earn a college degree. Our timing of the delivery was quite appropriate – Walter Cronkite offered his congratulations to us that evening!

It so happened that the television was on while I was preparing this summary on the Davis Quintuplets and a national news report stated that septuplets had just been born in Washington, D.C.[112] The head of the colossal team involved in this delivery was Craig Winkel, who had completed a fellowship in our department and was now Chairman of the Ob/Gyn Department at Georgetown University Medi-

[111] Dysmaturity – under development of fetal organs *in utero* (in the womb).

[112] Five boys and two girls were delivered by cesarean section on July 13, 2001 to a woman who asked to remain anonymous.

cal Center.   Our trainees continued to attain positions of prominence nationwide!

MEDICAL EMERGENCIES

Medical emergencies in which faculty and housestaff worked together were common.   Unlike many other Ob/Gyn departmental chairmen, I tried to stay in town in order to teach the residents by direct contact.   This, I found, often increased the knowledge of all involved, including me.   The following case is an example of this working relationship.

In 1959, the American Medical Association was meeting in Dallas.   Cesarean section was becoming quite popular and our department was invited to perform one on closed-circuit television.   I might have been guilty of hogging the spotlight, but nonetheless, I decided to be the surgeon with assistance from an excellent resident, Paul MacDonald. We had just admitted for a repeat cesarean section Betty Davis, a woman who had been delivered by this route twice before. She was thrilled to "be on television." Ms. Davis was legally an adult, and all the informed consent papers were signed. The television crew assembled the next morning and off we went – almost. At the last moment, Ms. Davis' mother demanded that her daughter not have surgery on camera. So we were left with hotels filled with doctors anticipating a live surgery – but now we had no patient.

We had admitted for cesarean section at that same time another woman, Winney Dorsey. She eagerly agreed to surgery on television and luckily she had not had breakfast. But wait. We confirmed that not only did she not have any living children, having previously delivered five stillborn infants, but at each delivery she hemorrhaged from abruptio placentae.[30] Previously in our research laboratory, we found that Ms. Dorsey had a chronic blood-clotting defect. Her plasma fibrinogen, measured as thrombin clottable protein, was abnormally low. Even so, we were still planning a cesarean section and hoping to avoid another fatal placental abruption and come out with a liveborn infant. As if matters were not complicated enough, the cameraman announced, "As soon as you cut we film the close-up. No matter what happens, we will continue filming until the operation is completed. We just recently filmed this same procedure at another meeting, and the operator slashed across the infant's nose. We continued filming through their attempts at repair. It was not pleasant!"

Things went very well. The healthy infant cried vigorously. Imagine, after five stillbirths Ms. Dorsey had a living, healthy baby! Some members of the audience even cried. Bleeding did not seem excessive immediately after delivery, but by 15 minutes or so postoperatively, all cut surfaces began to bleed and our concern rose. Vigorous fundal massage[113] plus oxytocin reduced the bleeding. We quantitated the blood loss and found it to be 1800 milliliters. This is twice the average blood loss from an otherwise uncomplicated repeat cesarean section and worrisome. A unit of blood was transfused though we probably did not need it.

We had had plenty of experience with blood loss associated with delivery and had measured it in a variety of circumstances with the following observations: Typical blood loss for an apparently normal vaginal delivery was 500 milliliters; blood loss with an apparently normal cesarean section was 1000 milliliters; and blood loss with an apparently uncomplicated cesarean hysterectomy was 1500 milliliters.[114] Obstetrics is a bloody business!

These average volumes of blood loss have since been confirmed. One military institution noted our results and decided to increase their recorded estimates to be compatible without actual measurements. The result was an investigation by the Inspector

---

[113] Fundal massage – massage of the belly.

[114] Pritchard JA, Wiggins KM, Dickey JC. Blood volume changes in pregnancy and the puerperium. I. Does sequestration of red blood cells accompany parturition? *Am J Obstet Gynecol.* 1960 Nov;80(5): 956-964.

Pritchard JA, Baldwin RM, Dickey JC, Wiggins KM. Blood volume changes in pregnancy and the puerperium. II. Red blood cell loss and changes in apparent blood volume during and following vaginal delivery, cesarean section, and cesarean section plus total hysterectomy. *Am J Obstet Gynecol.* 1962 Nov;84(10):1271-1282.

General to correct the high frequency of postpartum hemorrhage at this one hospital! Oh dear, more paperwork!

Our residents appreciated the contributions of the faculty and vice versa. Even though they often referred to me as "Black Jack", they obviously appreciated me at 4:00 a.m. one morning when I arrived in time to witness a woman in late pregnancy about to exsanguinate[115] from a ruptured uterus. On this occasion, an ambulance arrived with lights on and sirens blaring. The patient was dropped off in our emergency suite unaccompanied except for the driver who knew only where he had picked her up. When a family member was finally located, we learned that the patient was in late pregnancy and had previously undergone a cesarean section in another state. A doctor said he would deliver her at home since she had no money for hospital care.

Intravenous fluids – blood and Ringer's lactate solution – were infused rapidly through two intravenous lines. She soon became arousable as long as the two fluids were being pumped in. The dead fetus was removed with the placenta at laparotomy.[116] There was blood everywhere. As long as we vigorously administered fluids she maintained a measurable blood pressure. Dr. Doyce Dees appropriately performed a hysterectomy which helped control the bleeding. The incision was closed and the patient went to the recovery room where it was observed that her blood pressure was barely readable; and when moving her, we had lost the one patent intravenous line. A search for another one was futile. I remembered an exchange transfusion set with a large bore needle, and we gave it a try, puncturing her young healthy aorta and pumping a large volume of blood through it.

Once again, she became arousable, and her blood pressure was measurable but only as long as we pumped blood in. The culprit was an unligated uterine artery that was visible only while her blood pressure was reestablished. Pumping of blood continued, and her vi-

---

[115] Exsanguinate – be drained of blood, bleed to death.

[116] At laparotomy – at the time of laparotomy. Laparotomy – incision in abdominal wall.

tal signs were maintained. And we now had a new problem – stiff lungs from overtransfusing. Her hematocrit[117] was 63! With some difficulty we withdrew some blood to lower the hematocrit to the mid-40 range. The pulmonary embarrassment was relieved, and there was now minimal bleeding. Thanks to Dr. Skip Garvey from the Surgery department for his help treating the stiff lung problem.

We then compiled a list of all the possible serious complications that the patient might suffer from this horrendous ordeal. To have survived, she had obviously been in excellent health before the uterine rupture and massive hemorrhage. Relatively little damage was detected except for chronically impaired adrenocortical function[118] which was treated with hormonal replacement. The patient moved away but then moved back to the area she said to be able to obtain appropriate maintenance therapy from Dr. Paul MacDonald.

How long does one continue to treat massive hemorrhage in a pregnant or very recently pregnant woman? The above case of a ruptured uterus emptied our blood bank but does not hold the record for obstetric hemorrhage at Parkland. The record belongs to a woman who simultaneously had eclampsia and gross rupture of the liver. Her blood pressure was markedly elevated when she was first seen in the emergency room. She became hypotensive[119] before our eyes and the fetal heart rate very quickly became zero.

Dr. Gary Cunningham heard what was happening and quickly made the diagnosis of eclampsia plus rupture of the liver. The general surgeons had given up on her some time before and recommended that we do the same. After the transfusion of more than 200 units of blood and blood products, and many surgical procedures, Sandra Cody survived. When we last heard from Ms. Cody she was

---

[117] Hematocrit – proportion by volume of red blood cells in 100 milliliters of blood; normal range in women is 35–45 but the range can vary with lab.

[118] Adrenocortical function – impaired adrenal function as a consequence of obstetrical hemorrhage, possibly due to anterior pituitary infarction (tissue death).

[119] Hypotensive – patient had low blood pressure.

recovering from a fractured femur due to an ice skating mishap – in Texas!

One hot, muggy Dallas afternoon[120] as I was lecturing about the role of fibroids, someone opened the door, and we saw a large tornado coming our way. It was following the Trinity River bottom, moving from southwest to northeast. It veered close to St. Paul Hospital, through Exchange Park, and then down the main runway at Love Field. When it finally disappeared, there were a lot of casualties. I headed to emergency and found our resident arguing with the emergency room supervisor. I heard him say, "This woman has a ruptured ectopic pregnancy."

The supervisor, who was not one of my favorite people, blurted out, "You people in OB always want something! These emergency facilities are reserved for tornado victims only!" Slowly and steadfastly over time we had developed adequate operating facility for obstetrical emergencies. The resident and I moved the patient upstairs, scrubbed and draped her for surgery, and operated. It was a large, ruptured tubal pregnancy, and she needed the immediate care that we gave her. Amazingly, her name headed the list of tornado victims in the newspaper! We have since slowly but surely developed an adequate operating facility for obstetric emergencies.

As chairman, I had very little in the way of a private practice but what I did have tended towards the bizarre. After the successful pregnancy outcome in the woman with 5 fetal deaths from placental abruption, several women called wanting me to be their obstetrician. One had lost two children to placental abruption and was terrified throughout her third pregnancy. We delivered her by repeat cesarean section and baby and mother did fine. However, we could not get her to leave the hospital even though the home arrangements were most adequate. Finally, a clinic patient who had befriended her told her she could always sell the baby and then someone else could take care of the infant. She suddenly decided to go home and kept the baby. Follow-up indicated that once she was home she did admirably well.

---

[120] Tuesday, April 2, 1957.

Pritchard Family Photo

One 4th of July not long after arriving in Dallas, our family went water skiing. We arrived home nearly exhausted to find the telephone ringing off the wall. The caller was an obstetrician in the clinic group to which my friend from the Army belonged. In fact they had tried to recruit me for their new clinic.

He exclaimed that all but one of the clinical medical staff were celebrating the 4th, his wife was in shock and could I please come quickly. They assured me that it was not a ruptured ectopic pregnancy because she had marked bradycardia.[121] The internist thought it might be septic shock. They did not want to try to evacuate her to Dallas because she was "too ill."

I urged him to get at least two functioning IV lines in her and get some type-specific blood. A nurse anesthetist would be available. Still in my swim shorts and T-shirt, I rushed off to help with this case 60 miles away, all the while hoping I would not be stopped by a state highway patrolman.

The patient was cold, clammy, hypotensive,[119] stuporous,[122] and had a very slow pulse. I asked for the blood only to learn that it was on a Greyhound Bus somewhere between the blood bank in Dallas and Corsicana where the patient was. Her abdomen was distended, and I thought there was a fluid wave and a pelvic mass. A quick culdocentesis[123] was positive. Her hematocrit with both IV lines running was 18.[117] They had sterile bottles with anticoagulant ready

---

[121] Bradycardia – heart arrhythmia in which the heart beats too slowly.

[122] Stuporous – patient has a lowered level of consciousness.

[123] Culdocentesis – fluid is withdrawn from the pelvic cavity for examination.

to collect blood. We aspirated nearly 1000 milliliters of "blood" into two bottles after filtering it through sterile gauze, and infused it through the IV lines. In the meantime, the anesthetist achieved reasonable anesthesia, and I had the abdomen open.

Yes, it was a ruptured tubal pregnancy. Hemostasis[124] was promptly achieved, her vital signs became more favorable and after reassuring hemostasis, the lesion was resected and the abdomen closed. The hematocrit was now in the low 20s so we did not use the blood that was shipped much later via Greyhound. We had just recently reported on the absorption of red cells from the peritoneal cavity (Pritchard and Adams)[125] and knew that most of these cells would be eventually absorbed and survive normally. An important lesson learned from this case was that near exsanguination can be accompanied by severe bradycardia. Among my rewards for my trip to Corsicana: a plentiful supply of the world famous Corsicana, Texas fruit cake!

GYNECOLOGY

The Gynecology Service thrived. We had an abundance of gynecologic pathology whereas many other teaching centers were "running dry." Most all of the clinical faculty whenever called upon guided our housestaff through formidable operative procedures essential to good training. We asked the general surgeons to scrub in on gynecologic cases with a surgical component and vice-versa. Conflicts of interest were now minimal between these two services.

Cancer of the cervix was a troublesome gynecologic problem. It was being grossly over-diagnosed at times and under-diagnosed at others. We set up a cervical screening program to identify premalignancy and overt malignancy.

---

[124] Hemostasis – bleeding is stopped.

[125] Pritchard JA, Adams RH. Erythrocyte production and destruction during pregnancy. *Am J Obstet Gynecol.* 1960 Apr;79:750-757.

I spent 6 months during residency at Case Western Reserve Medical School working with one of the country's experts on cervical lesions as had Fred Bonte, our new Chief of Radiology. A new Pathology faculty member had also demonstrated excellent skills applicable to this challenge.

OB/GYN Archives

Jack A. Pritchard, M.D.—1973

We offered a cytologic smear (Pap smear) to every woman seen at Parkland Memorial Hospital for any complaint whether she was an outpatient or an in-patient, had appendicitis or a breast biopsy. A cervical smear was made by a trained technician and if a gross lesion was seen an "emergency" biopsy was done.

The incidence of cervical carcinoma rose markedly at first but fell precipitously as we identified and cured the majority of those identified with disease. The departments of Ob/Gyn, Radiology and Pathology continued to work compatibly. The rancor that had existed before I came to Dallas no longer prevailed.

Several organizations contributed to the funding of this project, and they were enthusiastic about the results we had achieved. We did such a good job that when the number of cases fell, they decided to fund other institutions who would follow our protocols. Once again, money played an important role in the provision of adequate medical care.

SOME UNUSUAL EVENTS IN MY CAPACITY AS A TEACHER

As I was leaving home for Love Field to fly to Chicago one day, a large car pulled across our driveway. An older, obviously upset man got out and started shouting at me. "You idiots have caused our family a lot of grief! One of your residents, somebody named Spier, told our son that if he did not do well in the Ob/Gyn program that he would have to repeat the course in a special summer session."

The angry father sent the taxi on its way and said he would drive me to Love Field. Each time he reached down below the steering wheel, I wondered if he had a gun stashed there. We arrived at the airport where I made a dash for the DC-7 as they were closing the doors. They left the ramp in place until I and my ticket got aboard, and then they locked up the plane and left the man behind.

The son had also complained to his father that in the middle of a case presentation I rudely stopped him and told everyone that I had heard enough. The case was an ectopic pregnancy that needed surgery right away! The father said that the downtrodden son was going to be a researcher and not practice clinical medicine. I did not try to convince him that his son should go into clinical medicine. I am also glad that Werner Spier did not have to enforce his threat of "If you goof off, you spend the summer in L&D." Actually, Dr. Spier was the student's best friend.

I have described elsewhere studies by Reuben Adams and me that demonstrated quantitatively the absorption of red blood cells from the peritoneal cavity into the blood stream. To do this we needed serial samples of the woman's blood. Surprisingly, most of our subjects were faithful about keeping their return appointments so we could obtain these blood samples. One patient, however, did not. So I suggested we track her down and draw the blood (with her permission, of course). My wife located her chart but the patient had no phone, so we went directly to her house in "Little Mexico."

I knocked on the door and a female voice said, "Come in." I entered and found a couple in a moderately advanced stage of foreplay. The woman held out her arm, I drew the blood and as I left, they resumed their prior positions!

A woman at one of the Ivy League schools wrote a book dealing with the difficulties that she had experienced in medical school and during residency training. I was the offender in one of her anecdotes.

As the story went, a professor in "a southwestern medical school" delighted in embarrassing women students. One day as he was lecturing the sophomore class on contraceptive techniques, he opened up boxes of condoms and diaphragms, inflated a few condoms and set them loose. Many of the students left their seats trying to catch one.

After a discussion of the advantages and disadvantages of the use of condoms, the professor emptied boxes of diaphragms and sailed several of them into the audience, exclaiming these could have been the Frisbees of his generation. Another flourish of activity as students tried to catch these mini-Frisbees. Levity was abundant. One sophomore woman student, however, was shocked by these actions during my presentation.

My son,[126] also a member of that sophomore class, told me not to worry about it. Most of the students felt that it was good education and an excellent presentation. Certainly one they would remember!

---

[126] David G. Pritchard—now an anesthesiologist in Las Cruces, NM—was a 1976 graduate of Southwestern Medical School.

SOME OTHER AWARDS AND HONORS

OB/GYN and UT Southwestern Library Archives
Jack and Signe Pritchard Fellowship in Maternal-Fetal Medicine—1985

This photo appeared on page 5 of the February 1986 issue of UT South-western's *Center Times*, along with an article entitled, "Fellowship honors Pritchards". Jerry Polley of Medical Illustration Services designed the plaque.

A most pleasant surprise for us came in my tenth year as Chairman of Ob/Gyn. We were given three pieces of beautiful luggage by Nieman-Marcus plus a plain envelope which contained an "unplain" gift – tickets for a trip around the world for Signe and me from our ex-residents! They appreciated the fact that I had received numerous offers to be the chair at many other prestigious Ob/Gyn departments but had elected to stay at Southwestern. Signe and I were humbled.

I received a few other accolades as time went on. The full-time Ob/Gyn and clinical faculty endowed the first Jack A. Pritchard Professorship[127] and later on the Jack and Signe Pritchard Fellowship in Maternal-Fetal Medicine.[128]

I am delighted that Gary Cunningham is the holder of the Jack A. Pritchard Professorship. The Pritchard fellowship is patterned after the fellowship that I was awarded at Case Western Reserve which helped finance the completion of my training before I accepted the Chair of Ob/Gyn at Southwestern. Susan Cox was the first Jack and Signe Pritchard Maternal-Fetal Medicine Fellow. An excellent choice!

After 25 years of service at Parkland and Southwestern, elegant saddlebags filled with silver bars were presented to Signe and me by Jerry McMahon as representative of all the ex-residents. So many wonderful gifts – we were in danger of becoming spoiled brats!

I deliberately describe these local awards before any of the national honors. I have long been convinced that a chairman ought to be appreciated first for his efforts "at home." If national recognition follows, that is fine. I have often said that I was much more interested in what the Chairman of the Department of Internal Medicine at Southwestern thought of the Ob/Gyn department than what the Chairman of Ob/Gyn at Harvard or Yale might think of us.

---

[127] The Jack A. Pritchard Professorship was endowed in 1975; Peggy Whalley was the first to hold the title. The endowment became the Jack A. Pritchard Chair in June 2004. Steven L. Bloom, M.D., Chairman of Obstetrics and Gynecology since 2006, currently holds the Pritchard Chair (2013).

[128] The Jack and Signe Pritchard Fellowship in Maternal–Fetal Medicine was established in 1985 when Dr. Pritchard semiretired.

Pritchard Family Photo

Jack A. Pritchard, M.D.
Distinguished Alumni Award—1997
Case Western Reserve University

I preferred to stay home and be an active participant in the wonderful laboratory that Parkland and Southwestern provided; however, a certain degree of national involvement was essential. I actively participated in the founding and development of the new National Institute of Child Health and Human Development (NICHD) which has had a profound effect on our expanding knowledge of reproductive biology.[129]

Johns Hopkins was one of several medical schools that gave us their stamp of approval not only by allowing the transfer of the authorship of *Williams Textbook of Obstetrics*, but also by later selecting a search committee that strongly favored either Paul MacDonald or me as candidates for the chair of their Ob/Gyn department. When I resigned the Chair to become the Chief of Obstetrics at Parkland and Paul MacDonald took over as Chair, Paul was happy, I was happy and the President of Southwestern was also happy. (Johns Hopkins, however, was not happy.) I continued to direct my attention to the establishment of the Greater Dallas Family Planning Project and began preparing for another edition of *The Bible*.

Other schools used a variation of the Johns Hopkins approach. For example, my *alma mater*, Case Western Reserve, sent two search committee members to Dallas to try to hire me back. They were also instructed to stay until I accepted. I did not accept, and Signe, my wife, finally sent them on their way. Years later (1997), Case Western Reserve bestowed on me the Distinguished Alumni Award.

It was a very real and exciting honor to receive the distinguished *Fellow ad Eundem* from the Royal College of Obstetricians and Gynaecologists in London.[130] The ceremony was very formal and Naren Patel (now <u>Sir</u> Naren Patel!) was my sponsor and presented me with the award. Before the ceremony, Signe asked Sir Naren if Jack should wear the 4-in-hand tie that Signe had in her purse rather

---

[129] Robert E. Cooke, M.D., chaired the 1961 taskforce that recommended the establishment of a new NIH institute to support research on human development and developmental disabilities. The NICHD was established by Congress in 1962. In 2008, the NICHD was renamed to honor Eunice Kennedy Shriver who had been an advocate for the Institute's founding. Dr. Cooke was the family's pediatrician and an advisor to President John F. Kennedy. http://www.nichd.nih.gov/about/overview/history/

[130] Dr. Pritchard was named *Fellow ad Eundem* in 1988.

than his beautiful silver bolo tie. He said, "No, everyone knows Jack by his bolo tie!" Thus the very formal picture of the group shows me in my bolo tie and lists my mailing address as Apache Junction, Arizona.

Royal College of Obstetricians and Gynaecologists Fellows ad Eundem Ceremony—1988

Pictured (back row, left to right) Professor Sir David Weatherall, Professor Ian Dawson, Professor Istvan Gati; (front row, left to right) Dr. Nafis Sadik, Professor Frederick Zuspan, Mr. George Pinker (President), Professor Kurt Swolin, Professor Jack Pritchard. Sir Naren Patel is not pictured.

Reproduced by kind permission of the Royal College of Obstetricians and Gynaecologists from the RCOG Photographic Archive, Reference RCOG/PH3/25.

Other honors which have been presented to me over the years include the following: President, Society for Gynecologic Investigation; Member, National Advisory Council of the National Institute of Child Health and Human Development; Committee on Maternal Nutrition of the National Research Council; Council on Food and Nutrition of the

American Medical Association; the Distinguished Scientist Award of the Society for Gynecologic Investigation (1988); Senior Author/Editor of *Williams Textbook of Obstetrics* for editions 14 through 17; and National Consultant to the Surgeon General of the Air Force (1968-90).

Editor's Addendum –

Dr. Pritchard was also the recipient of the Distinguished Service Award of the American College of Obstetricians and Gynecologists (1983).

OB/GYN Archives

Jack A. Pritchard, M.D.—1985

From 1966 until his retirement in 1990, Dr. Pritchard held the Gillette Professorship of Obstetrics and Gynecology.

Established by Mr. and Mrs. W. Everett DuPuy and the Fred G. Gillette or Maggie R. Gillette Foundation of Houston, the endowment was the first in the department. Dr. Fred G. DuPuy, the donor's son, was a 1963 graduate of Southwestern Medical School.

In 1985, Dr. Pritchard was named Ashbel Smith Professor of the University of Texas System. He was the second UT Southwestern faculty member to receive this honor; Morris Ziff was the first.

Established at UT Austin in 1963, the Ashbel Smith Professorship honored Dr. Smith who was the first chairman of the Board of Regents of the University of Texas.[131] The professorship was ex-

---

[131] Ashbel Smith was born in Hartford, Connecticut on August 13, 1805 and died at his plantation near present-day Baytown, Texas on January 21, 1886. He received his medical degree from Yale University in 1828. After coming to Texas in 1837, he became friends with Sam Houston and was appointed by Houston to the position of Surgeon General of the Republic of Texas Army. During the Mexican-American War (1846–1848), he served as Sur-

panded to include the faculty of the University of Texas Medical Branch at Galveston in 1964 and finally made available to each of the health components in 1980.   Upon retirement, holders of Ashbel Smith Professorships are entitled to use the title, "Ashbel Smith Professor Emeritus."

Dr. Pritchard also received the 1972 Marchman Award from the Dallas Southern Clinical Society "in recognition of his development of an outstanding academic department and for his own important contribution to research and his development of a Planned Parenthood program in this region."

On November 28, 2001, Dr. Pritchard was honored by friends and colleagues at a reception sponsored by the UT Southwestern Obstetrics and Gynecology Alumni Association. It was his last visit to UT Southwestern. The photograph of him in the section – In Closing – and those below were taken by David Gresham at that event.

OB/GYN Archives – David Gresham, Photographer
Drs. Jack A. Pritchard and F. Gary Cunningham

geon General of the U.S. Army. During his final term in the Texas House of Representatives, he focused on establishing a liberal arts university in Austin (1883) with a medical branch in Galveston (1891) near his home.

OB/GYN Archives – David Gresham, Photographer

Drs. Jack Pritchard, Uel Crosby, and Rigoberto Santos–Ramos

OB/GYN Archives – David Gresham, Photographer

Drs. Joe Godat, Pritchard, and Walter "Ben" Hogan

OB/GYN Archives – David Gresham, Photographer
Drs. Susan Cox and Jack Pritchard

OB/GYN Archives – David Gresham, Photographer
Drs. Jack Pritchard and Karen Bradshaw

OB/GYN Archives – David Gresham, Photographer

Dr. Alvin "Bud" Brekken, Signe Pritchard, and Dr. Jack Pritchard

OB/GYN Archives – David Gresham, Photographer

Signe and Jack Pritchard

OB/GYN Archives – David Gresham,
Photographer

Jack Arthur Pritchard, M.D.
November 28, 2001

IN CLOSING

Since the time when the sperm and egg fused in 1920 to give life to Jack A. Pritchard, unbelievable advancements have been made in the understanding of human reproduction. Along the way, roadblocks of most every type and description have occurred.

Nonetheless, I do believe I would choose to travel this road all over again given the opportunity as long as I had the help of my wife, Signe, and all my wonderful colleagues.

I am deeply indebted to Lynne McDonnell for assistance in the typing and editing of this manuscript.

Jack A Pritchard MD

There is an innumerable list of people who I worked with until my retirement in 1990 and who contributed greatly to the growth of the Department of Obstetrics & Gynecology. Below are only a few of these wonderful people:

Gary Ackerman	Joe Godat	Bill Miller
Reuben Adams	Richard Goldstein	Hamp Miller
Wayne Agnew	Clark Griffith	James Muse
Mark Akin	Gary Hankins	David Partlow
Ken Armstrong	John Hauth	John Pickel
Bill Baker	Hugh Haynes	Jim Richards
Richard Baldwin	Steve Heartwell	Susan Ramin
Mark Bernstien	David Hemsell	Charles Rolle
John Bertrand	Robert Hirsch	Bernie Rothschild
David Bookout	Ben Hogan	David Russell
James Boyd	Charles Hung	Bill Rumsfeld
Karen Bradshaw	Gene Hunt	Rigoberto Santos
Alvin Brekken	John Jeffers	A. Schindler
Charlie Brown	Juan Jimenez	Barry Schwarz
Barbara Cambridge	Joe Johnson	M. Schultz
J.T. Christmas	Robert Kuhne	Dan Scott
Bob Cluck	Larry Laufer	James Scott
Blue [Frank C.] Council	Kenneth Leveno	Dick Sparr
Susan Cox	Scott Livesay	Werner Spier
Uel Crosby	Tom Lowe	Stuart Stone
Gary Cunningham	Mike Lucas	Jim Strong
Bob Darrow	Mark Maberry	Ken Talkington
Doyce Dees	Charles Martin	Doug Tatum
John Dickey	Fran Martin	Ali Toofanian
Noble Doss	Jerry Martin	Judy Wagers
Johann Duenhoelter	Joe Martin	George Wendel
Fred du Puy	Craig McCoy	Gene White
Clare Edman	Jack McCubbin	John P. Wood
Walter Evans	Jerry McMahon	

Marvin Gerard	Bruce Meek	And many, many,
Larry Gilstrap	Bill Midget	many more!

Jack and Signe Pritchard—circa 2001

Jack Arthur Pritchard, M.D., died in Las Cruces, New Mexico on May 28, 2003. He was survived by his wife of 58 years, Signe, and his three sons—Jack Allen, David George, and Allen Jeffrey.

Epilogue

When he arrived in Dallas, Dr. Pritchard found a department that very much resembled the shacks it called home. William F. Mengert, Chairman 1943–1955, had laid out a blueprint for how the department should be organized. But, organization alone does not make a department. And in 1955, Dr. Mengert's department was disintegrating around him – consumed by the conflict with radiology over who would treat cervical cancer.

Jack Arthur Pritchard breathed life into the Department of Obstetrics and Gynecology. He gave it purpose and a culture, and introduced it to evidence-based medicine. He _built_ the department!

As you read Dr. Pritchard's story, you realize that an equally fascinating story is unfolding right beside it – the story of Signe Allen Pritchard. Throughout his career, Signe was at his side. Whether with tape measure, patient chart, or in the library looking for references, she shared in Dr. Pritchard's professional life. It was also Signe who encouraged him to write his life story. And, it was Signe who was instrumental in getting it published.

There were no "little people" or "extras" to Jack _or_ Signe Pritchard. Each person had a contribution to make and collectively these individual contributions made up the entity that was – and still is – the Department of Obstetrics and Gynecology.

It's no surprise that Dr. Pritchard singled out the talents of Robert Wright, Gwen Chase, and Ruble Mason; nor that he acknowledged the administrative abilities of Juanita Epperson. He appreciated what people did.

Signe was his ambassador of thanks. When a secretary had done an exceptional job or "gone above and beyond", Signe would hand out gold stars. Corny? Perhaps. But it worked! This simple gesture simultaneously acknowledged the contribution and "connected" the administrative staff to the mission.

Now, living in Las Cruces, New Mexico, and about to celebrate her 89th birthday, Signe Allen Pritchard is still handing out gold stars. With thanks to Signe, I'd like to share the one I received recently with you.

— Judy Wagers
September 1, 2012

Aug 6 – 2012

My dear Judy,

Oh my goodness, you have done an exceptional job with this manuscript, taking it from a worthwhile piece of memorabilia to a publishable form. As I read it and reread it, I cried in places and laughed in others as it brought back so many memories. I know Jack never envisioned it to be published but I know deep in my heart that he would be pleased. Thank you, Judy Wagers.

Fondly,

Signe

After receiving a paperback of *Every Life Has A Story And This Is Mine* for her 90th birthday, Signe enthusiastically agreed to, "Publish it!" With thanks to Signe for her encouragement and love, I share her comments with you.

Dec. 15, 2013

My dear Judy,

Oh Oh Oh my, Jack's book is stunningly beautiful. I knew if you did this project that it would be done with heart and soul to make it a keeper, and you did.

Fondly,

Pritchard Family Photo

Jack Arthur Pritchard in the Superstition Mountain Wilderness near his Apache Junction, Arizona home.

The mountain in the background is Weaver's Needle.

About the Author and Editor

JACK ARTHUR PRITCHARD, M.D., graduated from Case Western Reserve University with an M.D. degree in 1946. He completed a fellowship in Pharmacology at the same institution and contemplated getting a Ph.D. His enthusiasm for obstetrics and gynecology was reawakened during a year of active military duty in Japan, and he completed his residency in that specialty after discharge. In 1955, Dr. Pritchard became the second Chairman of Obstetrics and Gynecology at UT Southwestern Medical Center in Dallas, Texas. He held this position until 1970 when he became the senior author/editor for *Williams Obstetrics*. Dr. Pritchard continued to practice and teach at UT Southwestern until his full retirement in 1990. In 2001, at the urging of his wife, Signe, he wrote his autobiography, *Every Life Has A Story And This is Mine*.

ഉര

JUDY ANNE WAGERS, editor of *Every Life Has A Story And This Is Mine*, has master's degrees in both English and business administration. She began her professional career as an editor and project manager for a California publisher of children's educational materials. In 1973, she joined the Department of Obstetrics and Gynecology at UT Southwestern Medical Center in Dallas, Texas, where she met Dr. and Mrs. Pritchard. Since her retirement as the department's business manager in 2009, she has been writing about the history of the department for the UT Southwestern website. This project led to her editing Dr. Pritchard's autobiography. In 2013, Judy and her scientist husband, Robert, published the book, *Mysteries of the Marfa Lights Revealed* — the culmination of their seven-year investigation of "mysterious" light phenomena seen near the west Texas town of Marfa.

ഉര

Made in the USA
Middletown, DE
07 February 2020